REMEMBRANCES, RESIDENCES, RECIPES, and a FAMILY TREE

Connie Erickson Rosenquist

REMEMBRANCES, RESIDENCES, RECIPES, AND A FAMILY TREE

iUniverse books may be ordered through booksellers or by contacting:

iUniverse
1663 Liberty Drive
Bloomington, IN 47403
www.iuniverse.com
1-800-Authors (1-800-288-4677)

Because of the dynamic nature of the Internet, any web addresses or links contained in this book may have changed since publication and may no longer be valid. The views expressed in this work are solely those of the author and do not necessarily reflect the views of the publisher, and the publisher hereby disclaims any responsibility for them.

Any people depicted in stock imagery provided by Thinkstock are models, and such images are being used for illustrative purposes only.
Certain stock imagery © Thinkstock.

ISBN: 978-1-4917-4808-4 (sc)
ISBN: 978-1-4917-4809-1 (hc)
ISBN: 978-1-4917-4807-7 (e)

Library of Congress Control Number: 2014917224

Printed in the United States of America.

iUniverse rev. date: 11/14/2014

My Swedish heritage and the lush and beautiful lake-filled country of Finland, birthplace of my grandparents and father, have always been an inspiration.

This cookbook is dedicated to

my mother Celia,

for her expertise in the kitchen in cooking and in design,

my maternal grandmother Nana,

for her hors d'oeuvres, Swedish coffee bread and pies,

and

my husband Bob, sons Erik and Kris, and daughters-in-laws Laura and Toni whose encouragement and technical expertise made this cookbook possible.

Introduction

I wrote this book for several reasons. Breakfasts, lunches, and dinners prepared by my Swedish mother—and hors d'oeuvres and pies by my Swedish grandmother—have given me great pleasure throughout my life and I treasure these memories. In my twenties I prepared meals for my husband and sons, voraciously reading *Gourmet* and later *Food & Wine*.

Dinners with friends in both California and Maryland where we lived from 1969–1973 expanded my palate. By the 1980's, I had time to follow my interest in contemporary art, serving as president of Art Alliance, the support group of the art department at California State University Fullerton, and then as president of the Oakland Museum of California Art Department's support group, Art Guild. I was privileged to co-lead art day tours and extended trips, always researching cutting edge restaurants in the various destinations. I have loved discovering exciting new chefs, but treasure preparing meals for friends and family in my own home even more.

Cookbooks have come and gone, but presently my collection includes 104. Many recipes included in *Remembrances, Residences, Recipes, and a Family Tree* were discovered in these cookbooks. I also love good movies and recommend five films with a culinary theme. You may come to like them as much as I did. They are *Ratatouille, Like Water for Chocolate, Chef, Tortilla Soup,* and the Scandinavian treasure, *Babette's Feast.*

Contents

Appetizers

Berkeley, California

*A man travels the world over in search of what
he needs and returns home to find it.*

—George Moore

*The feeling of being "at home" is the feeling of belonging. It is the
history that clings to remembered objects ... when a childhood
memory is dislodged by a chance encounter with the past.*

—Linda Weltner

Holiday Snowman

Makes 3 1/4 cups

This cheese ball makes a unique centerpiece for a holiday party. It is from the *Children's League Hors d' Oeuvres Cookbook.*

2 (8-ounce) packages cream cheese
3/4 pound Roquefort cheese, crumbled
2 tablespoons finely grated onion
1 teaspoon prepared mustard
1 tablespoon Worcestershire sauce
dash Tabasco sauce
black olives
carrot sliver
pimento-stuffed olives
parsley sprigs
celery slivers

Early in the day, combine cream cheese, Roquefort cheese, onion, mustard, Worcestershire sauce, and Tabasco sauce. Cover and refrigerate for 1 hour. Shape 1 3/4 cups of cheese mixture into a large ball. Set it on a pie plate. Next, shape 1 cup of mixture into a second ball. Set on top of the first ball. Shape remaining cheese mixture into a ball and pace on top of the second ball. Refrigerate.

About 1 1/2 hours before serving, reshape snowman balls, if necessary. From ripe black olive, cut 2 rounds; press into the head for eyes. From the carrot sliver, pare a nose. Use pimento stuffing from olive for mouth; press into place. Add parsley sprig for hat. Slice a stuffed olive and use for buttons on snowman's coat. Use celery slivers for arms. With broad spatula, remove snowman to a serving tray. Surround with parsley. Refrigerate until serving.

Have crackers and spreaders nearby.

Erik's Cottage Cheese Rounds

Makes 18

This recipe is from the 1962 *Sunset Dinner Party Cookbook*. The appetizer has been enjoyed by our family since the 1960's, particularly over holidays.

    1 cup flour
    1/2 cup soft butter
    1 cup small curd cottage cheese
    1 teaspoon salt
    1 egg yolk, beaten

Sift flour; measure, and combine in a bowl with all ingredients except yolk. Blend well. Shape into a ball, and knead 10 times on a lightly floured board. Roll to 1/2 inch thick and cut into rounds 1 1/2–2 inches in diameter. Brush tops with beaten egg yolk. Bake on greased baking sheet at 450 degrees until lightly browned, 12–15 minutes. Serve hot.

Parmesan Trees

Makes 24

The "trees" are an easy hors d'oeuvre to prepare and children like them. The trees are similar to an hors d'oeuvre made by Nana at Christmas and Thanksgiving in the 1950's and 1960's.

3/4 cup Parmesan cheese, grated
1/2 cup mayonnaise
1/4 teaspoon ground white pepper
2 tablespoons onion, grated
24 slices white sandwich bread

Preheat oven to 400 degrees. In a small bowl, combine all ingredients except bread. Lay bread on a work surface and cut with a tree-shaped cookie cutter. Spread about 2 teaspoons of cheese mixture evenly onto each tree. Arrange trees on baking sheet and bake 5–7 minutes until golden and bubbly. Serve immediately.

Hobbits

Makes 24

The recipe reminds me of an appetizer served at The Hobbit, a restaurant in Orange. It was a hit at many cocktail parties before Children's League's festive "Snowball."

  1 package Pepperidge Farm frozen puff pastry shells
  6 ounces salami, thinly sliced
  8 ounces Monterey jack cheese, thinly sliced

Unwrap shells and place 3 (one on top of another) shells on a smooth surface. Roll 4-inches square. Transfer to a baking sheet. Cover with salami and cheese. Roll out remaining 3 shells in similar manner and cover layers. Bake according to directions on package. Cut into squares and serve immediately.

Spiced Pistachios

Makes 2 cups

This is from Saratoga's Sent Sovi, made for Erik and Laura's second holiday party.

   1/4 cup sugar
   1/2 teaspoon salt
   1 tablespoon curry powder
   2 teaspoons ground coriander
   1/2 teaspoon ground cumin
   1/8 teaspoon cinnamon
   1/8 teaspoon ginger
   2 tablespoons olive oil
   2 cups unsalted shelled pistachios

Line a shallow baking pan with parchment paper. In a small bowl, stir together sugar, salt, and spices. Cook pistachios in oil in a 12-inch skillet over moderate heat, stirring occasionally until a shade darker, about 5 minutes. Stir sugar mixture into nuts, and cook over moderate heat, stirring constantly until sugar begins to melt and coats nuts evenly, about 2–3 minutes. Transfer nuts to baking pan and cool.

Spinach-Leek Dip

Makes 3 cups

Fullerton friends Roger and Carol Burtner served this dip before dinner at one of our American Association of University Women movie group evenings.

1 package frozen chopped spinach
1 package Knorr Leek Dip
1 cup sour cream
1 cup mayonnaise
1 can water chestnuts, chopped
1 (6 1/2-ounce) can clams, drained and minced
Assorted crackers

Thaw and squeeze all moisture out of the spinach. Stir all ingredients together. Chill overnight. Serve with crackers.

Pico de Gallo Dip

Makes 2 cups

Blue tortilla chips are excellent with this dip. I first enjoyed it at Gloria's apartment on Prince Street in Oakland.

1 small tomato, coarsely chopped
1/4 cup cilantro, coarsely chopped
1 (8-ounce package) cream cheese, softened
2 tablespoons jalapenos, coarsely minced
1/3 cup onion, finely chopped
1/4 teaspoon salt
blue tortilla chips

Pulse all ingredients in a food processor until smooth. Transfer to a serving bowl. Chill, covered, until slightly thickened, about 1 hour.

Fire and Spice Nuts

Makes 6 cups

Addictive! They will stay fresh one week in an airtight container at room temperature.

 2 teaspoons Chinese 5-spice powder
 2 teaspoons cinnamon
 2 teaspoons ground ginger
 2 teaspoons salt
 3/4 teaspoon chili powder
 3/4 teaspoon garlic powder
 1/4 cup sugar
 2 large egg whites
 2 cups walnut half pieces
 2 cups cashew half pieces
 1/2 cup crystalized ginger, cut into matchstick pieces

Position racks in top and middle of oven. Preheat oven to 225 degrees. Line two heavy cookie trays with parchment paper. Stir in first seven ingredients in small bowl to blend. Whisk eggs in a large bowl until foamy. Whisk in spices. Add nuts and toast. Sprinkle with sugar and toss to coat. Divide nut mixture between the two baking pans, spreading in a single layer. Bake until nuts are toasted and coating is dry, stirring every 20 minutes for 1 hour and 20 minutes. Salt nuts to taste. Transfer to a bowl and toss with ginger. Cool.

Chèvre Grapes

Serves 8

I have taken this appetizer to my book club and served it at private dinners. It is always popular.

1 bunch seedless red grapes, about 1/2 pound, stems removed
1 6–8 ounce log unflavored goat cheese
small amount half and half, if needed
3/4 cup pistachios, shelled
coarsely ground pepper to taste

Wash and thoroughly dry grapes. Add a small amount of cream to cheese to make pliable. Wrap each grape with a thin layer of cheese and set on a rimmed sheet. Lightly toast nuts at 350 degrees for about 10 minutes, being careful not to burn. Cool. Grind nuts in a food processor, being careful not to pulverize. Spread nuts on a plate; turn the cheese-covered grapes in the nuts, coating lightly. Refrigerate covered for at least 20 minutes, but not more than 4 hours. Garnish with ground pepper.

Prosciutto with Lemon and Dill

Makes 24

An easy appetizer, first served in the Napa Valley at Trefethen Vineyards.

24 thin slices prosciutto
1 tablespoon fresh dill, minced
1 teaspoon lemon zest, minced
2 limes, cut into thin wedges

Roll prosciutto into a cylinder. Mix dill and lemon zest. Sprinkle over prosciutto. Serve with lime wedges.

Avocado Blender Crab (ABC Dip)

Serves 8

This dip is from *After Five*, published by Fullerton's Children's League.

1 large avocado, peeled
1 tablespoon lemon juice
1 tablespoon grated onion
1 teaspoon Worcestershire sauce
1/4 cup sour cream
1 (8-ounce) package cream cheese, softened
1/4 teaspoon salt
7 1/2-ounce can crab, drained (fresh crabmeat is even better)

In a blender, combine avocado, lemon juice, onion, and Worcestershire sauce until smooth. Add sour cream, cream cheese, and salt, blending well. Stir in crab. Chill and serve with crackers.

Smoked Salmon Bundles

Serves 6

This delicious appetizer is from *Outdoor Dining*, a cookbook published in 1995.

    1 avocado, halved with pit removed
    1 clove garlic, finely chopped
    1/2 small red onion, finely chopped
    juice of half a lemon
    1/2 teaspoon Tabasco sauce
    6 slices smoked salmon
    blanched chives for garnish

To make guacamole, scrape flesh of the avocado into a bowl. Add garlic, onion, lemon juice, and Tabasco sauce. Mash mixture with a fork. Cover with plastic wrap and refrigerate until ready to use.

For the bundles, lay slices of smoked salmon on a board. Place a spoonful of guacamole on each slice. Fold salmon over guacamole mixture. Tie each parcel with blanched chives. They may be halved.

Cheddar Pennies

Makes 2 dozen

This hors d'oeuvre from the Children's League's cookbook *After Five* is good to have in the freezer for unexpected guests.

1/2 cup (1 cube) butter, softened
3 tablespoons onion soup mix, crushed
1/4 teaspoon salt
1 cup sifted flour
1/2 pound sharp cheddar cheese

Combine all ingredients, mixing thoroughly. Shape into rolls about 1-inch thick. Wrap in foil and freeze. When ready to use, slice into 1/8-inch thick rounds. Place on a cookie sheet. Preheat oven to 375 degrees. Bake for 10 minutes.

Goat Cheese Avocado

Serves 6

City Restaurant, a favorite of Karl's in Los Angeles, is one of the many Wilshire cafes he introduced to Bob and me.

4 ounces Montrachet soft goat cheese
1/2 cup olive oil
herbs for marinade (such as basil, thyme, rosemary, peppercorns)
salt to taste
4 ripe avocados, halved and pitted
juice of 1 lemon
4 dashes Tabasco sauce
1/8 teaspoon white pepper
salt to taste

Marinate goat cheese in olive oil at room temperature in a small covered container for at least a day. Herbs such as basil, thyme, rosemary, and peppercorns may be added. Before serving, lift cheese out of oil. Combine with avocados, lemon juice, Tabasco sauce and pepper in a large bowl. Mash with a fork until mixture is slightly lumpy, not a smooth purée. Season sparingly with salt. May be offered cold with chips or warm on baguette slices.

Guacamole I

Serves 6–8

I made this in 1997 at Erik and Laura's Los Gatos home when Bob's best friend from Cal and best man in our wedding George Watson and his wife Elaine came to meet our first grandchild, Marin.

3 ripe avocados
1 fresh jalapeno, stemmed and seeded
1/2 white onion, diced
1/4 cup cilantro, coarsely chopped
juice of 1 lime
1/2 teaspoon salt
black pepper, freshly ground
1 ripe tomato, seeded, diced and chopped
lettuce leaf (optional)
corn tortilla chips

Cut each avocado lengthwise into quarters, removing the pit. Peel off skin and place pulp in a bowl. Using a potato masher, mash lightly. Add jalapeno, onion, cilantro, lime juice, salt, pepper to taste, and diced tomato. Mix just until combined, with avocado chunks visible.

To serve, spoon guacamole into a serving bowl. If not serving immediately, poke the avocado pits down into the center of the mixture to prevent discoloration. Cover tightly with plastic wrap and refrigerate up to 4 hours. Serve chilled with tortilla chips.

Petite Cream Puffs

Makes 2 dozen

Fill with tuna, chicken, or egg salad. The puffs may be made 1 day ahead, but not stuffed.

> 1 cup water
> 1/2 cup butter
> 1/2 teaspoon salt
> 1 cup sifted flour
> 4 eggs

Put water, butter, and salt into a heavy 1-quart saucepan. Heat to boiling; reduce heat to very low. Add flour all at once. Stir with wooden spoon until mixture leaves sides of pan, looks dry, and forms a ball. Remove from heat. Add eggs one at a time, beating well after each addition. Beat until smooth and velvety. Drop 3/4-teaspoon balls on ungreased baking sheet. Bake at 400 degrees for minutes until puffs are dry. Cool on rack. Carefully cut off top of each puff.

Radish Canapés

Makes 24

Bob loves radishes, and this easy but delicious appetizer disappears quickly. It is from Lee Bailey's book, *California Wine Country Cooking*, published in 1991.

    1 loaf homemade-style white bread, sliced medium thin
    1/4 cup (1 stick) unsalted butter, softened
    2–3 bunches red radishes
    fresh chives, finely chopped

Cut the bread into 2 1/2-inch rounds with a cookie cutter, making 24 in all. Spread each round generously with softened butter. Slice the radishes thin and arrange on bread in concentric circles. Sprinkle with chopped chives. Lightly cover with a damp cloth and keep chilled until ready to serve.

Marin's Guacamole II

Serves 6

Our granddaughter is a superb guacamole maker. She varies the recipe each time she makes it. This is her favorite version.

4 ripe avocados
1 bunch cilantro, chopped
6-7 garlic cloves, halved
2 tablespoons chopped red onion
1/2 large jalapeno, seeded and diced
1 lime, cut in half
sea salt to taste

Peel avocado and mix in food processor. Add 2/3 of cilantro, garlic, onion, jalapeno, the juice from half a lime, and sea salt to taste. Blend well. If desired, add more cilantro, jalapeno and/or sea salt. Make sure avocado still has a few lumps. Put in a bowl and cover with plastic wrap. Place in the refrigerator for no longer than 1 hour, until serving.

Miniature Frittatas

Makes 24

This is another good recipe from *Outdoor Dining*.

4 ounces smoked salmon, finely chopped
3 ounces crumbled goat cheese
fresh chives, chopped
6 eggs
1/4 cup light cream

Grease two mini-muffin tins. Divide smoked salmon, goat cheese, and chives between tins. Lightly beat eggs with cream; pour over salmon mixture. Bake at 400 degrees for 8–10 minutes or until golden brown. Turn onto a wire grill to cool. Serve at room temperature.

Potato Skins

Serves 8–10

Bob and I were introduced to these at TGI Friday's in Costa Mesa. We enjoyed a drink there with our friends Ann and Doug Myles after our Saturday matinees at South Coast Repertory.

    12 small baking potatoes
    1/2–1 cup (1–2 cubes) butter, melted
    1/2 cup vegetable oil
    ¼ cup chopped green onions
    1-2 teaspoons onion powder or garlic salt
    1/2 pound bacon, cooked and crumbled
    12 ounces cheddar cheese, grated
    1 (8-ounce carton) light sour cream

Preheat oven to 300 degrees. Wash potatoes and rub with oil. Bake for 1 hour; remove from the oven. Cut potatoes in half lengthwise and let cool. Scoop out centers, reserving for mashed potatoes for another meal. Brush potato skins with melted butter. Before baking, sprinkle skins with chopped green onions and either onion or garlic salt. Bake at 300 degrees for 20 minutes. Sprinkle bacon and cheese on skins. Return to oven for 5 more minutes. Serve with sour cream.

Erik's Onion Rings

Serves 6–8

We ask Erik to make these, as his recipe is the best ever.

    4 medium red onions, very thinly sliced
    1/2 cup buttermilk
    1 cup flour
    1–2 teaspoons salt
    1 cup vegetable oil
    1 teaspoon black pepper

Soak onion rings in buttermilk for 1 hour. Take rings out of the buttermilk and drop into a bag filled with flour, salt, and ground pepper. Shake. Fry in oil until brown and crisp, about 3 minutes. Drain on paper towels. Serve hot, adding salt if needed.

Fried Green Olives

Serves 6

This appetizer is great on New Year's with Domaine Chandon Brut. Janet and I ordered it as an appetizer at Berkeley's Downtown.

1 ounce mild blue cheese (such as Maytag)
24 pitted Spanish olives, patted dry
all-purpose flour
1 large egg, beaten
1 cup dry breadcrumbs or Panko crumbs
½ cup olive oil

Roll small amount of cheese into log shape. Stuff olives with cheese. May be made one day ahead. Cover and chill. Pour enough oil into heavy large skillet to measure depth of 1 inch. Heat. Roll stuffed olives in flour, egg, and breadcrumbs to coat. Fry olives until golden brown, about 30 seconds. Using a slotted spoon, transfer to paper towels to drain. Serve hot.

Greek Cheese in Olive Oil and Herbs

Serves 6

When unexpected guests arrive, this is quick and easy to prepare.

1/2 pound feta cheese
olive oil
fresh or dried oregano
red pepper flakes, crushed
1 package pita bread
olive oil
salt

Place a 1 x 4-inch piece of drained feta cheese on a small plate. Drizzle olive oil over the top and around the sides. Sprinkle oregano and crushed red pepper flakes over the top.

Serve with pita crisps. To make crisps, preheat oven to 400 degrees. Cut one package of pita bread into quarters. Arrange triangles with the rough sides up on a baking sheet and drizzle with olive oil. Sprinkle with salt. Bake for 10 minutes or until lightly browned. (They can burn easily.)

Parmesan Pine Nut Crackers

Makes 5 dozen

I found this recipe in Peggy Knickerbocker's cookbook, *Simple Soirées*. It may be prepared the day before.

- 2 cups flour
- 1/2 teaspoon salt
- dash of cayenne
- 1 cup (2 sticks) unsalted butter
- 1 pound Parmigiano-Reggiano cheese, grated
- ¾ cup pine nuts

Sift flour and salt. In another bowl, sprinkle cayenne over butter and cream together, adding 1 cup of cheese at a time until well blended. Add flour mixture, blending well. Shape the dough into 3 logs, 1–1½ inches in diameter. Wrap the logs in plastic wrap, and chill until firm.

Preheat oven to 400 degrees. Cut logs into 1/4-inch slices. Place on ungreased baking sheets, leaving a 1/2 inch between the slices. Press a whole pine nut into the center of each slice. Bake for about 8 minutes or until light brown. Watch very carefully as they can burn easily. Cool on wire rack.

Fennel-Marinated Feta
and Kalamata Olive Skewers

Yields 24 skewers

These were a real winner at Erik and Laura's 2007 holiday party at Shadow Bend. They are labor intensive, but well worth it.

2 tablespoons sesame seeds
2 teaspoons finely grated orange zest
3 tablespoons fresh orange juice
1 teaspoon cracked black peppercorns
A 5 ounce feta cheese block, diced into twenty-four-inch cubes
24 fresh mint leaves
12 pitted Kalamata olives, halved
1/2 cucumber, peeled, seeded and cut into a 1/4-inch pieces
24 6-inch skewers

In a medium bowl, combine sesame seeds, zest, juice, and pepper. Gently stir in the feta cubes and marinate for 1 hour at room temperature or u to 3 hours in the refrigerator

To assemble the skewers, push a mint leaf about 3/4 inch up the skewer. Add a chuck of cucumber and an olive half. Gently place a cube of the feta on the end.

Parmesan Puffs

Serves 6

This hors d' oeuvre, popular in the 1960's and similar to Nana's recipe, is having a renaissance.

1 cup Parmigiano-Reggiano cheese
1/2 cup mayonnaise
1 tablespoon onion, minced
1/8 teaspoon cayenne
9 slices white bread, crusts removed

Preheat oven to 400 degrees. Mix cheese, mayonnaise, onion, and cayenne in a medium bowl. Set aside.

Cut four circles or squares from each slice of bread. Arrange pieces on a baking sheet and bake for 3–4 minutes, or until toasts are crisp and golden. Cool the toasts and top each with 1/2 teaspoon of cheese mixture, spreading to the edge of the toasts. Put toasts back in the oven and bake for about 6 minutes, or until the tops are puffed and golden. Remove from the oven and serve warm.

Baked Artichoke Dip

Serves 10–14

Artichokes were the first crop at the Rosenquist & Copley ranch in Salinas.

1 cup mayonnaise
3/4 cup sour cream
2 cups grated Parmesan cheese, divided
3 tablespoons cider vinegar
2 tablespoons chopped fresh basil
2 cloves garlic, minced
1 teaspoon kosher salt
1 teaspoon ground black pepper
1 (13 1/2-ounce) can artichoke hearts
1 bell pepper, roasted, peeled, and diced
1 (7-ounce) can diced green chilies, drained
tortilla chips

Preheat oven to 350 degrees. Combine mayonnaise, sour cream, 1½ cups cheese, vinegar, basil, garlic, salt, and black pepper. Gently fold in artichokes, bell pepper, and chilies. Transfer to a baking dish. Scatter remaining 1/2 cup cheese over the top. Bake uncovered until lightly browned, 45 minutes. Remove from oven. Cool for 5 minutes. Serve with tortilla chips.

Marinated Olives

Serves 12–14

Bob likes marinated olives, and we often choose different types at Andronico's on Solano Avenue. I found this interesting recipe.

grated zest of half an orange
grated zest of half a lemon
2 cloves garlic, minced
1 cup chopped flat-leaf parsley
1/4 cup chopped fresh cilantro
2 tablespoons chopped fresh rosemary
2 tablespoons fresh oregano
1 teaspoon peeled fresh ginger, minced
1 teaspoon kosher salt
1 teaspoon ground black pepper
1/2 teaspoon red pepper flakes
1/2 teaspoon fennel
2 cups extra-virgin olive oil
4 cups assorted olives, drained (Nicoise, Kalamata, and Picholine)
1 1/2 teaspoons white truffle oil (optional)

In a food processor, combine the orange zest, lemon zest, garlic, parsley, cilantro, rosemary, oregano, ginger, salt, black pepper, red pepper flakes, and fennel. Process until thoroughly blended, 1–2 minutes. Add the olive oil and pulse briefly to incorporate into the herb mixture.

Put the olives in a bowl and pour the herb mixture over them. Add the white truffle oil, if desired. Toss to combine.

Transfer to a large serving bowl and serve. You may store the olives, submerged in the olive oil, in tightly capped jars in the refrigerator for up to 1 month.

Smoked Salmon Mousse

Serves 6

Timberline Lodge was built in 1936 by skilled WPA (Works Progress Administration) craftsmen. The *Timberline Lodge Cookbook* is the source of this recipe.

1 pound cream cheese
6 ounces smoked salmon
1/4 cup butter, melted
juice of half a lemon
1/4 cup heavy whipping cream
4 tablespoons capers
2 teaspoons prepared horseradish
pinch of white pepper

Whip the cream cheese in a mixer until soft. Slowly add the remaining ingredients. Whip until smooth. Chill until firm, approximately 1 hour.

Chill at least 1 hour. Serve with crackers or raw vegetables.

Cheddar Gougères

Makes 4 dozen

This recipe is from the November 2013 *New York Times*. I made the appetizer before Thanksgiving dinner and everyone loved it.

> 6 tablespoons unsalted butter
> 1 teaspoon salt
> 1 cup sifted flour
> 5 large eggs
> 1 cup sharp cheddar cheese

Place 1 cup water in a 2-quart saucepan. Add butter and salt. Simmer just until butter melts. Remove from heat, add flour all at once and stir vigorously. Return saucepan to medium heat and cook dough, stirring one minute. Transfer dough to a food processor.

Heat oven to 425 degrees. Turn on food processor and add 1 egg to the dough. As soon as it is completely incorporated, add another, and continue adding eggs one at a time until you have used 4 eggs. Add cheddar cheese, and pulse to blend.

Line one large or two small baking sheets with parchment. Drop teaspoons of batter in mounds about 1 inch across on baking sheets, leaving 2 inches between. Beat remaining egg. Brush tops of mounds with egg, taking care not to let any drip down the sides.

Bake 15 minutes until puffed and lightly browned. Reduce heat to 350 degrees and bake another 10–15 minutes, until well browned. Shut off oven, open door a few inches, and leave gougères another 15 minutes before removing them. When completely cooled, the gougères may be transferred to a heavy plastic bag and frozen. Reheat them for 10 minutes at 350 degrees.

Ham and Rye Fritters

Makes 24

Lee Bailey is the creator of this appetizer. He has written nine cookbooks, all of them excellent. The recipes are easy to follow. The fritters were served at a champagne dinner at Schramsberg Vineyards & Cellars in the Napa Valley.

    1 cup whole milk
    1/2 stick (1 cube) unsalted butter, cut into small cubes
    1/2 cup rye flour
    1/2 cup all-purpose flour
    3 eggs
    1 ounce Monterey Jack cheese
    3 ounces smoked ham, diced into small pieces
    1 teaspoon caraway seeds

Preheat oven to 425 degrees. Heat milk and butter in a saucepan until butter is melted and mixture boils. Sift flours over medium heat, stirring constantly. Continue to cook and stir butter until it leaves the sides of pan and forms a ball, 1–2 minutes. Remove the pan from stove. Off the heat, beat in eggs one at a time. Beat in the cheese, ham, and caraway seeds. Form dough into 24 balls, 1 inch in diameter. Place 2 inches apart on a greased cookie sheet. (If dough is not firm enough to form into balls, chill for 30 minutes.) Bake for 15 minutes. Reduce heat to 325 degrees and bake for an additional 10–15 minutes, until golden.

Beverages

Visalia, California

To be happy at home is the ultimate result of all ambition ...

—Samuel Johnson

Cambria, California

The house shelters daydreaming, protects the dreamer,
and allows one to dream in peace.

—Gaston Bachelard

Millennium Cocktail

Makes 1

I will always remember enjoying this libation with Karl and Bob the hours before 2000 began.

    1 1/2 ounces Courvoisier
    1 1/2 ounces pineapple juice
    1/4 ounce orange Curacao
    2 dashes bitters

Mix in large shaker. Pour over ice.

Old Fashioned

Makes 1

My parents ordered this drink in the 1950's. The drink was created in Kentucky circa 1900 for a retired Civil War general who didn't care for the taste of straight whiskey.

    1/2 orange slice, cut about 1/4 inch thick
    1 maraschino cherry, stem removed
    3 dashes bitters
    1 teaspoon water
    1/2 teaspoon superfine sugar
    2 1/2 ounces VO or other fine bourbon

In a 6-ounce Old Fashioned glass, combine the orange slice, cherry, bitters, water, and sugar. Mix the ingredients with the back of a teaspoon to dissolve sugar and mash the fruit somewhat. Fill the glass with ice cubes, add the bourbon, and stir gently.

Minted Grapefruit or Champagne Cooler

Serves 6

The cookbook *California Cooking* by the Los Angeles County Museum of Art was a gift from Christian Neighbors when I resigned in July 1988 to care for my father. Bob and I enjoyed this recipe with Jon and Shirley in Lancaster.

3 1/2 cups freshly squeezed grapefruit juice
2 tablespoons sugar
6 sprigs mint
6 tablespoons freshly squeezed and strained lemon juice
3 1/2 cups champagne or ginger ale

Combine the grapefruit juice, sugar, and mint in a pitcher. Let mixture sit overnight. Just before serving, add lemon juice and champagne or ginger ale. Fill glasses with ice cubes and pour in the liquid mixture. Garnish with fresh mint and serve immediately.

Boulders Sunrise

Makes 1

A morning beverage from the luxurious Arizona resort, the Boulders, north of Sedona, where Bob and I stayed twice. Karl loved the desert. Our graduation present to him when he earned his PhD from UCLA was a stay here.

1 cup fresh orange juice
1 tablespoon honey
1/4 cup fresh lime juice
pinch of nutmeg

Stir first three ingredients together and top with nutmeg.

Sazerac

Erik, Karl, Bob, and I tasted this drink in New Orleans when we celebrated Thanksgiving in the early 1990's. I enjoyed it at Roux in San Jose, listening to Erik's band "Big Horn Rex" play.

2 teaspoons Pernod
1/2 teaspoon superfine sugar
3 dashes Peychaud's bitters
1 teaspoon water
2 1/2 ounces bourbon
lemon twist

Pour Pernod into a 6-ounce Old Fashioned glass and swirl to coat the glass; pour out any excess. In another Old Fashioned glass, mix the sugar, bitters, and water with the back of a teaspoon until the sugar is dissolved. Fill the first glass with crushed ice. Add the bourbon to the mixture and stir gently; pour into the ice-filled glass. Rub the outside of the lemon twist around rim of the glass, twist over the glass to release the oils, and drop it into the drink as a garnish.

Sidecar

Makes 1

Bob made this drink in Sacramento in 1961, the year Erik was born. It was created at Harry's Bar in Paris during World War I. We had a lemon tree with the sweetest fruit.

    2 tablespoons triple sec, divided
    sugar to coat the rim of the glass
    2 ounces brandy
    1 tablespoon fresh lemon juice

Refrigerate glass for 1 hour. Pour 1 tablespoon triple sec onto a small plate. Invert the glass and twist the rim in the triple sec to moisten. Dip the rim in sugar coating lightly. In a cocktail shaker two-thirds full of ice cubes, combine the brandy, 1 tablespoon triple sec, and lemon juice. Shake well and strain into the glass.

Black Russian

Makes 1

I first had this drink at the Plaza Hotel in New York City in early December 1961 when I was traveling with Bob to a chemical engineering conference. It was our first trip to the Big Apple.

1 1/2 ounces vodka
3/4 ounce Kahlua

Place ice cubes in an Old Fashioned glass. Pour in vodka, then Kahlua. Stir gently and serve.

Aquavit Bloody Mary

Serves 6

On a visit to New York City in 1991 with three Art Alliance friends, one dinner was at Aquavit, whose award-winning Swedish chef was Marcus Samuelson. The restaurant's name is the same as the Scandinavian liquor, Aquavit. I learned to like it on a trip to Sweden and Finland in 1998. My Fullerton friend Shirley Bloom and I were traveling companions. We also visited Denmark and Norway.

    1 cup Aquavit, chilled
    1 quart V-8 juice
    3 tablespoons fresh lemon juice
    2 tablespoons Worcestershire sauce
    1/2 teaspoon Tabasco sauce
    1/4 teaspoon black pepper
    salt to taste
    lemon slices and small celery ribs

Stir together all ingredients with salt to taste in a pitcher. Serve over ice in six highball glasses. Garnish with lemon slices and small celery ribs.

Pimm's Cup

Bob was introduced to this drink in London on a trip to Germany and England with his parents after his Cal graduation in 1958. I had it at Five Crowns in Costa Mesa in about 1965.

    1 ounce Pimm's No. 1
    1/2 cup ginger ale
    slice of lemon
    slice of cucumber

Pour the Pimm's No. 1 and ginger ale into a chilled glass over ice. Squeeze the lemon slice as you drop it into the glass. Stir gently. Garnish with the cucumber slice.

Irish Coffee

Makes 1

This recipe originated at San Francisco's popular Buena Vista. Bob and I first enjoyed one my senior year at Cal in 1959. We now have this libation at Brennan's in Berkeley. My grandmother Nana bought turkey sandwiches for us when we came to Berkeley from Sacramento in 1960.

6 ounces brewed coffee
2 sugar cubes
1 1/2 ounces Bushmills whiskey
lightly whipped cream

Fill an Irish coffee glass with very hot water to pre-heat, then empty it. Pour hot coffee into hot glass until it is about three-fourths full. Drop in 2 cocktail sugar cubes. Stir until the sugar is thoroughly dissolved. Add the whiskey and top with a dollop of cream.

Margarita

Makes 4–6

Bob and I first enjoyed this drink from "south of the border" in about 1973 at a restaurant in the Villa del Sol on Harbor Boulevard in Fullerton. We had moved back to California to 3800 Rosehedge Drive after four years at 320 Linwood Avenue in Bel Air, Maryland.

  1 cup gold tequila
  1 cup Cointreau
  1 cup fresh lime juice, plus lime wedges or additional juice
  1/4 cup superfine sugar
  Kosher salt for dipping glass rims
  6 cups ice cubes

In a blender, combine the tequila, Cointreau, 1 cup lime juice, and sugar. Cover and process on high speed until the sugar dissolves and the mixture is thoroughly combined, about 10 seconds.

Spread a layer of salt on a small flat plate. Rub the rim of a glass with a lime wedge, or dip the rim in lime juice. Then dip the rim into the salt to coat lightly. Repeat with the remaining glasses. Fill each glass three-fourths full with the ice. Pour in the blended mixture, filling almost to the rim. Place a narrow wedge of lime on top and serve at once.

Pisco Sour

Makes 1

Karl told us about this drink after his trip to Machu Picchu. I enjoyed it again in San Francisco at La Mer with Bob, Kris and Toni, Alexander and Erikson in summer 2011.

    1 egg white
    6 ounces pisco
    2 ounces fresh lime juice
    1–2 ounces Simple Syrup (recipe is below)
    2 cups crushed ice
    Angostura bitters

Place egg white in a blender and blend briefly, until frothy and light. Add all the other ingredients except the bitters, and blend until frothy and smooth. Adjust with more citrus or sugar as needed. Pour into two glasses and sprinkle with a drop or two of bitters.

Simple Syrup

This recipe, an ingredient in the Pisco Sour above and in the Ramos Fizz, is from Susan Spicer's *Crescent City Cooking*.

    1 cup sugar
    1 cup water

Heat sugar and water in a small saucepan over medium-low heat, stirring occasionally until sugar melts. Allow the syrup to cool and then store in the refrigerator.

Ramos Gin Fizz

Makes 1

Bob and I first had this on our fifteenth wedding anniversary in 1975. My parents gave us a Caribbean cruise, staying with Erik, Karl, and Kris in Fullerton for the week.

 2 ounces gin
 1 1/2 ounces half and half
 1/2 ounce Simple Syrup
 2–4 drops orange flower water
 1 1/2 ounces orange juice
 splash of fresh lime juice
 soda water, as needed
 orange slice

Combine all ingredients except soda water and orange slice in a cocktail shaker with crushed ice. Shake vigorously. Strain into a chilled class, and top with enough soda water to fill the glass. Garnish with an orange slice.

Fizz facts. A classic gin fizz is made with gin, fresh lemon juice, sugar, and soda. It is traditionally served in a tall glass over ice. Stirring in a frothy egg white changes it into a Silver Fizz, and adding orange flower water and cream makes it a Ramos Gin Fizz, a drink created in the 1880s.

Breakfast and Brunch

Lodi, California

The country of our childhood survives, if only in our minds.

—Laurie Colwin

Lorell's Blender Pancakes

Serves 4

This easy recipe is from *Charleston Receipts Repeats*, a cookbook I purchased in this beautiful Southern city in 1988 on a Thanksgiving visit to Karl.

 4 eggs
 1 cup small curd cottage cheese
 1 1/2 cups sour cream
 1 cup flour
 1 teaspoon salt
 1/2 teaspoon baking soda
 1 tablespoon sugar (optional)

Combine eggs, cottage cheese, and sour cream in a blender. Combine flour, salt, and baking soda (may add 1 tablespoon sugar) and add to blender, mixing well. Pour on a greased griddle in desired size.

My Mother's Waffles

Serves 6

This waffle recipe, also from *Charleston Receipts Repeats,* is one of Bob's favorites. He likes cheese added.

2 cups flour
1 1/2 teaspoons salt
4 eggs, separated
2 cups milk
8 tablespoons (1 cube) butter, melted
2 heaping teaspoons baking powder

Sift flour and salt. Beat egg yolks. Add milk and flour alternately. Beat in melted butter. Add baking powder. Fold in beaten egg whites. Pour batter onto a greased griddle. Repeat.

Gingerbread Pancakes

Serves 6

I first tasted gingerbread pancakes in 1953 as a counselor for Tri-Hi-Y at Camp Tulequoia near Sequoia National Park. I recently made them for my grandchildren and they love them. This recipe, from Magnolia Cafe in Charleston, was in *Gourmet*'s December 2006 issue.

    2 cups flour
    1 teaspoon baking soda
    1/2 teaspoon baking powder
    1/2 teaspoon salt
    1/4 teaspoon cloves
    1 teaspoon cinnamon
    1 teaspoon ginger
    1 1/2 teaspoons nutmeg
    3 eggs
    1 1/4 cup firmly packed brown sugar
    1/2 cup buttermilk, well shaken
    1/2 cup water
    1/4 cup brewed coffee (not espresso)
    6 tablespoons unsalted butter, melted and cooled
    vegetable oil

Preheat oven to 200 degrees. Whisk together flour, baking soda, baking powder, salt, and spices. In another bowl, whisk together eggs and brown sugar until smooth. Whisk in buttermilk, water, and coffee until combined. Whisk in melted butter.

Heat a dry griddle over moderate heat until hot enough to make drops of water scatter over surface. Brush with vegetable oil. Working in batches, fill a 1/4-cup measuring cup with batter for each pancake, then pour onto griddle and cook, turning over once, until deep golden (about 2–3 minutes per batch.) Transfer to a heatproof platter and keep warm in an oven until ready to serve.

Crème Fraiche Pancakes

Makes 3 dozen

This is another winner from Lee Bailey! It is similar to Nana's Swedish pancakes, but easier.

    4 large eggs
    1/2 teaspoon salt
    1 teaspoon baking soda
    1/2 cup all-purpose flour
    2 tablespoons sugar
    2 cups crème fraiche
    2 tablespoons unsalted butter, melted
    vegetable oil
    syrup or jam

Place all ingredients except butter and oil into a blender. Blend until smooth. Pour in butter. Stir once to make sure everything is mixed.

Grease a well-heated griddle with vegetable oil. Pour out 1/4 cup batter. When bubbles on top burst, turn pancakes. Continue, greasing griddle as needed. Serve with syrup and/or jam. Crisp bacon is a good accompaniment.

Eggs Ortega

Serves 6

One of my mother's favorites. In the 1950's, using Ortega chilies in cooking was a rarity.

    1 1/2 pounds Jimmy Dean pork sausage
    1 dozen eggs
    3/4–1 cup milk
    salt and pepper to taste
    2/3 small can Ortega green chilies
    1/2 cup grated cheddar cheese

Cook sausage and pour off fat. Beat eggs with milk. Add salt and pepper. Combine green chilies with egg mixture. Pour into pan with cooked sausage and stir to proper consistency.

Spanish Omelet

Serves 5–6

Sausage lovers adore this recipe!

1 pound linguiça sausage, sliced
1 can diced tomatoes
1 1/2 cups cheddar cheese, diced
1/2 onion, diced
3 tablespoons oil, divided
6 eggs
salt and pepper to taste

Fry linguiça; pour off grease. Add tomato, minus the juice, cheese, and onion. Simmer until most of juices are absorbed. Put 2 tablespoons of oil into a large fry pan. Beat 6 eggs. Salt and pepper to taste. Add 1 tablespoon hot oil to eggs. Cook over medium heat until eggs are done. Pour tomato mixture on one side of eggs. Fold one-half of eggs over the top. Let sit 30 seconds. Cut into wedges.

Cream Cheese and Chive Scrambled Eggs

Serves 8

These eggs were served at Erik and Laura's engagement party in Berkeley in 1992. We met Laura's parents Les and Jill and her grandmother Helen for the first time.

16 large eggs
8 ounces cream cheese, cut into bits and softened
2 tablespoons minced chives
2 tablespoons unsalted butter
Salt and pepper to taste
Garnish with more chives and a rolled piece of smoked salmon

Whisk together eggs, cream cheese, chives, salt and pepper to taste. In a large skillet, melt butter over moderate heat. Add egg mixture and cook, stirring for 6–8 minutes or until the eggs are cooked. Serve eggs sprinkled with chives and a piece of salmon.

Cheese and Leek Puff

Serves 6–10

This is from *California Heritage Cookbook*. Toni made it for a May 2008 brunch for fellow kindergarten teachers.

    12 slices sour dough, standard loaf
    6 tablespoons butter
    1 pound sharp cheddar cheese, grated
    8 tablespoons diced leeks, white part only
    8 eggs
    4 cups milk
    1 1/2 teaspoons dry mustard
    1 1/2 teaspoons salt
    pepper to taste
    2 teaspoons Worcestershire sauce

Remove crust from bread; then butter and cut into 1-inch cubes. Place on the bottom of a lightly greased 13 x 9 inch casserole. Spread cheese on top of bread and sprinkle with the leeks. In a large bowl, combine the eggs, milk, mustard, salt, pepper, and Worcestershire sauce, mixing well. Pour the mixture over the cheese. Cover and refrigerate overnight.

The following day, remove the casserole and let stand at room temperature for 30–60 minutes. Preheat oven to 350 degrees and bake for 30–40 minutes, or until lightly browned and puffed. Eat immediately.

Breakfast Popovers

Serves 6

This recipe from *Gourmet LA* is a fun addition for a breakfast or brunch.

6 eggs
2 cups flour
2 cups milk
1/2 teaspoon salt
4 tablespoons butter, melted
2 cups Swiss cheese
2 cups lean diced ham

Preheat oven to 400 degrees. Combine eggs, flour, milk, salt, and butter in a blender. Blend until frothy. Oil twelve large popover cups. Place cheese and ham in cups, dividing evenly. Pour the batter over the cheese, filling cups 3/4 full. Bake 35–40 minutes, until browned. Remove from cups and serve immediately. Batter may be prepared ahead and refrigerated. If using chilled batter, add 5 minutes to baking time. Once popovers are cooled, keep in a sealed plastic bag overnight. Re-crisp at 375 degrees for 5 minutes.

Fabulous French Toast

Serves 6–8

From *A Taste of Palm Springs*. Bob and I attended the Indian Wells tennis tournament for many years. Karl, Erik, Kris, and Toni shared time there with us. I loved watching Stefan Edberg.

4–6 eggs, slightly beaten
1 cup whole milk
2 teaspoons vanilla
1 teaspoon cinnamon
1/2 teaspoon salt
1 loaf egg bread, unsliced
Butter and peanut oil, equal parts

Mix all ingredients except bread in shallow dish. Slice bread 1 inch thick and soak in egg mixture 15 minutes. Heat oil and butter to high temperature and fry bread until golden on both sides.

Cardamom Sour Cream Waffles

Serves 4

This recipe uses my favorite Scandinavian spice, cardamom.

1 1/2 cups all-purpose flour
1 1/2 teaspoons baking powder
3/4 teaspoon baking soda
1/4 teaspoon salt
1 teaspoon cardamom
1 cup whole milk
1 cup sour cream
1 teaspoon vanilla
1 tablespoon mild honey
2 large eggs
2 tablespoons unsalted butter, melted
3 tablespoons unsalted butter

Preheat waffle iron. Meanwhile, whisk together flour, baking powder, baking soda, salt, and cardamom. In another bowl whisk remaining liquid ingredients, including melted butter. Add to flour mixture until just combined. Brush waffle iron with butter and bake waffles.

Layered Omelet

Serves 12

This recipe is a bit time consuming, but not difficult. It is from LACMA's *California Cooking*.

Note: The spinach, leek, and tomato mixtures may be prepared a day ahead and chilled overnight. Do not cook eggs or assemble until just before baking.

> 1 pound trimmed spinach, or 1 package frozen spinach,
>   defrosted and chopped
> 11 tablespoons butter, divided
> freshly ground nutmeg, to taste
> salt
> pepper, freshly ground
> 1 cup leeks (white part), finely chopped
> 1/4 pound Brie, chilled
> 3 tomatoes, peeled and seeded
> 1/2 teaspoon thyme
> 24 eggs
> 1/4 cup heavy whipping cream
> watercress sprigs, for garnish

Cook spinach in water until wilted. Drain and squeeze dry. In a skillet, heat 3 tablespoons butter. Add spinach, nutmeg, salt, and pepper. Cook until moisture has evaporated. Transfer to a bowl.

Wipe out skillet. Heat another 3 tablespoons butter to sauté leeks until softened. Season with salt and pepper. Transfer to a bowl and set aside. Scrape the rind from the Brie and thinly slice. Set aside.

Wipe skillet and heat 3 more tablespoons butter. Sauté tomatoes, stirring occasionally until moisture has evaporated. Add thyme. Salt and pepper to taste. Transfer to another bowl and set aside.

Preheat oven to 375 degrees. Butter bottoms of loaf pans (12 x 4 x 2 1/2 inches each) and line with parchment.

Whisk eggs with 1 teaspoon salt and pepper. Set aside 1 cup of eggs. Divide the rest evenly between two bowls. Put 2 tablespoons butter in a skillet, softly scrambling eggs. Transfer to a plate.

Repeat with the remaining butter and eggs. Combine the reserved 1 cup eggs with cream. Pour one-third of mixture into each prepared pan. Layer half the scrambled eggs, a fourth at a time, with half each of spinach, leeks, Brie, and tomatoes ending with scrambled eggs. Pour remaining egg-cream mixture over the tops, letting it seep down around the layers.

Cover pan with buttered parchment paper. Put the loaf pans in two larger baking pans and add enough hot water to reach halfway up the sides. Bake the omelets for 35–40 minutes until set. Let sit for 5 minutes. Remove parchment paper and invert onto serving platters. Remove the remaining parchment paper. Let stand for about 10 minutes to facilitate slicing. Serve warm, garnished with watercress.

Surprise Breakfast Casserole I

Serves 8–10

A popular brunch dish from the 1970s for holiday mornings.

   8–10 slices sour dough bread, crusts removed
   1 pound Jimmy Dean hot sausage
   1/2 cup chopped celery
   1/2 cup chopped green pepper
   1/2 cup chopped Ortega mild chilies
   2 tablespoons grated onion
   4–5 eggs, slightly beaten
   3 cups milk
   1 can cream of mushroom soup
   1 1/2 cups grated Monterey jack cheese

Line bottom of 9 x 13-inch pan with 4–6 slices bread. Brown sausage and add it and vegetables to baking dish. Cover with remaining bread. Mix eggs and milk and pour over casserole. Refrigerate overnight. Bake at 325 degrees for 45 minutes. Remove casserole and cover with the soup. Sprinkle cheese over the top and return to oven for 15 minutes more.

Brunch Eggs California II

Serves 8

May be made the night before serving. The recipe is from Los Angeles Jr. League's 1988 cookbook *Gourmet LA.*

Eggs

2 cups fresh corn, about 2 ears
2 tablespoons butter
12 eggs
1/2 cup milk
1 1/2 cups sour cream
1 tablespoon Worcestershire sauce
4 cups cheddar cheese, shredded
1 teaspoon salt
1/2 teaspoon pepper
8 ounces green chilies, diced

Sauté corn in butter for 5 minutes, until tender. Cool. Beat eggs. Add remaining ingredients, mixing well. Add corn. Pour into oiled 9 x 13-inch baking dish. Bake 1 hour 15 minutes at 350 until firm and golden on top. Serve with sour cream, tomatoes, guacamole, and Salsa Fresca.

Salsa Fresca

2 ripe tomatoes
1/2 onion
1/4 cup chopped green bell pepper
3 cloves garlic
2 teaspoons juice of pickled hot chili peppers
1/4 cup chopped cilantro
salt to taste
1 1/2 cups tomato juice

Combine tomatoes and onion in a food processor. Pulse until coarsely chopped. Add bell pepper, garlic, and juice of peppers. Pulse 2–3 times. Add cilantro, salt, and tomato juice. Pulse. Refrigerate.

Prosciutto and Goat Cheese Strata III

Serves 6

Erik and Laura found this recipe in the December 2003 issue of *Bon Appetit*. A good way to begin the day!

18 slices firm white bread (i.e. English muffin bread)
6 ounces prosciutto, thinly sliced
8 ounces crumbled goat cheese
4 ounces (1 1/2 cups) grated provolone
1/4 cup chopped green onions
6 tablespoons julienned basil
6 large eggs
2 cups whole milk
1 tablespoon Dijon mustard
1/2 teaspoon salt
3 tablespoons melted butter

Line bottom of 13 x 9 x 2-inch glass baking dish with one layer of bread, cut to fit. Arrange half of prosciutto evenly over bread. Sprinkle half of goat cheese and half of provolone over bread. Sprinkle with half of green onions and half of basil. Top with second layer of bread. Layer remaining prosciutto, goat cheese, provolone, green onions, and basil. Top with remaining bread, cut into 4-inch cubes.

Whisk eggs, milk, mustard, and salt in a bowl. Season with pepper. Pour egg mixture over strata; press down on bread with a spatula. Drizzle melted butter over strata. Cover and refrigerate overnight. Preheat oven to 350 degrees. Uncover strata and let stand at room temperature for 30 minutes. Bake until center is set, about 1 hour. Remove from oven. Preheat broiler. Place strata under broiler until top is golden, about 30 seconds. Cut into large squares and serve.

Swedish Pancakes

Serves 3–4

This recipe was given to me by my father's cousin Elna Josephson when Bob and I were first married. Her mother and Papa's mother were sisters.

  3 eggs, separated
  2 tablespoons sugar
  1/4 teaspoon salt
  4 tablespoons melted butter
  1/2 cup flour
  1 1/2 cups milk
  lingonberry jam
  maple syrup

Beat egg yolks with sugar, salt, and melted butter. Stir in the flour and milk alternately, mixing well. Let stand. Whip egg whites. Fold the whites into the yolk mixture, leaving lots of air where possible. Spoon out onto buttered griddle to cook. Serve with lingonberry jam or maple syrup.

Easy Cottage Soufflé

Serves 6

From *A Pinch of Salt Lake*, a cookbook I purchased at the Denver Airport en route to a Thanksgiving in New Orleans.

6 eggs
16 ounces small curd cottage cheese
1 pound Monterey Jack cheese
1 cup Bisquick
1/2 cup unsalted melted butter, divided

Preheat oven to 350 degrees. Beat eggs in a medium bowl. Add cottage cheese and Monterey Jack cheese, blending well. Stir in Bisquick and ¼ cup melted butter. Place 1/4 cup butter in a soufflé dish. Add the egg and cheese mixture. Bake for 45–60 minutes.

German Hotcakes

Serves 6

Bob's grandmother, Louise ("Weeze" to our children), made them for Betty, Butch, Judy, and him when they were little, always serving "boys first." She later prepared them for Bob and me in her Bradley home in Monterey County. Today, Butch makes them on his outside grill in Lockwood. Toni prepares them for Kris, Alexander, and Erikson in Portland.

> 3 eggs
> dash of vanilla
> dash of salt
> 3 cups whole milk
> 1/4 cup flour or a little more, if needed
> 6 teaspoons butter, divided

Mix all ingredients. Melt a teaspoon of butter into a 10-inch crepe pan, a flat pan, or onto a grill. Surface must be very hot. Pour enough batter into pan to cover. Cook until edges are browning, and turn. Slide out onto a warm platter. Follow the same pattern, beginning with the melting of a teaspoon of butter. Good with warm syrup.

Spicy Oven Omelet with Chile Cheese Sauce

Serves 12

This recipe is from *A Taste for Comfort* cookbook. We stayed at Channel House in Depoe Bay with Kris the night before his graduation from OSU. Kris and Toni have spent special times there.

18 eggs
1 cup sour cream
1 cup whole milk
1 cup cottage cheese
1 4-ounce jar pimentos, chopped
1/2 cup diced green chilies
1 cup shredded Monterey Jack cheese
2 tablespoons unsalted butter, divided

Sauce

3 tablespoons unsalted butter
3 tablespoons all-purpose flour
1 cup whole milk
1 cup shredded smoky cheddar cheese
1/4 cup diced green chilies

Preheat oven to 350 degrees.

Mix eggs, sour cream, milk, and cottage cheese. Stir in pimentos, chilies, and Monterey jack cheese. Place 1 tablespoon butter into each of two 9-inch round cake pans and melt. Pour egg mixture into pans; bake for 45 minutes or until firm. Cool 10 minutes before slicing.

For Sauce

While omelet is baking, melt butter in heavy saucepan. Stir in flour; let bubble for 30 seconds. Whisk in milk, cooking until thickened. Stir in cheese and chilies. Serve over omelet wedges.

Lemon Craisin Popovers with Lemon Honey Butter

Makes 12

These popovers are served at another of our favorite Oregon inns, Tu Tu' Tun Lodge on the Rogue River. Bob and I first stayed here in the summer of 1998 with Ina on a trip en route to Portland.

2 cups all-purpose flour
1/2 cup craisins (dried cranberries)
2 cups whole milk
4 eggs
1/4 teaspoon salt
2 teaspoons finely grated lemon rind

Lemon Honey Butter

1/2 cup butter
2 tablespoons honey
2 teaspoons lemon juice
2 tablespoons grated lemon rind

Preheat oven to 425 degrees. Whisk together flour, craisins, milk, eggs, salt, and lemon rind. Batter will be slightly lumpy. Butter twelve 6-ounce popover pans. Fill two-thirds full with batter. Bake 30–35 minutes until puffed and browned. Serve with lemon honey butter.

For Lemon Honey Butter

Beat butter until smooth. Whip in honey, lemon juice and lemon rind.

Breads

Bradley, California

An old farm is always more than the people under
its roof. It is the past as well as the present.

—Henry Beston

Focaccia

Serves 8

We have enjoyed this delicious bread at Erik and Laura's Shadow Bend home in the hills above Los Gatos.

2 (1/4-ounce) packages or 5 teaspoons yeast
1 teaspoon sugar
2 cups warm water
1 tablespoon salt
5 1/2 cups all-purpose flour, divided
1/3 cup olive oil
2 teaspoons minced thyme
2 tablespoons cornmeal, divided
1/2 cup coarsely grated parmesan cheese
black pepper and salt, for sprinkling

Mix yeast, sugar, and water, and let stand 5 minutes, or until foamy. In a bowl stir together salt and 5 cups flour. Stir olive oil into yeast mixture. Gradually add flour mixture to yeast mixture. Knead dough until soft and slightly sticky. Transfer dough to a floured surface and knead in enough remaining flour to form a soft but not sticky dough. Form dough into a ball and put in an oiled large bowl, turning to coat. Cover bowl with a kitchen towel and let dough rise in a warm place until doubled in bulk, about 45 minutes. Transfer dough to a lightly floured surface and divide in half. Knead thyme into one half and knead plain half, 1 minute. Form each half into an oval and invert bowl over them. Let dough rest, 5 minutes for easier rolling.

Preheat oven to 450 degrees. Oil two 13 x 9-inch baking pans and sprinkle each with 1 tablespoon cornmeal. On lightly floured surface, roll out dough halves into 12 x 9-inch rectangles and fit into pans. Cover each pan with a kitchen towel and let dough rise in a warm place until doubled in bulk, about 20 minutes. Bake for 12 minutes or until golden. Drizzle with a good olive oil and serve.

Banana Bread

Makes 1 loaf

This is from my AOII sorority house on Prospect Avenue at Cal. We had a wonderful deck looking over the Bay Bridge and San Francisco.

    1/2 cup Crisco
    1 cup sugar
    1 teaspoon salt
    2 eggs
    3 bananas, mashed
    1 teaspoon soda
    1/4 cup hot water
    2 cups flour
    1/2 cup chopped walnuts

Mix Crisco, sugar, and salt. Add remaining ingredients. Bake at 375 degrees for 1–1 1/4 hours.

Cheese Wafers

Makes 32

The cheese holds its own with the flavor of sorrel. (See Soups)

1 cup grated Swiss cheese
1/4 cup grated parmesan cheese
1/2 cup (1 stick) unsalted butter, softened
1 teaspoon salt
1/2 teaspoon ground white pepper
1 cup all-purpose flour

Preheat oven to 350 degrees. In a large bowl, cream the cheeses and butter. Stir in salt and white pepper. Mix flour in thoroughly until you can make a ball. Divide dough in half, then keep dividing in half until you have 32 small balls, rolling them with your hands. Place the balls about 2 inches apart on an ungreased cookie sheet. Flatten slightly. Bake for 15 minutes, or until golden. Remove with a spatula to a rack. Serve immediately.

Easter Pigeons

Erik and Karl loved to help make these. The recipe is from the 1963 *Sunset Breads* cookbook. They were a highlight on three Easter mornings at my parents' ocean house in Cambria.

1 3/4 cups milk
1 package yeast
1/4 cup warm water
1/3 cup sugar
2 teaspoons salt
2 eggs, beaten
3-4 cups sifted flour, divided
1/2 cup melted butter

Scald milk and cool to lukewarm. Dissolve yeast in warm water and add to the lukewarm milk. Add sugar and salt. Stir in beaten eggs. Gradually add 2 cups of the flour, beating until smooth. Add melted butter and mix well. Add enough extra flour to make a soft dough.

Turn out on a lightly floured board and knead lightly. Cover with a cloth and let rest 15 minutes. Knead again until smooth and elastic. Put in a greased bowl, cover, and let rise in a warm place until almost double in bulk, about 1 hour. Punch down dough and roll out on a lightly floured board to a 1/2-inch thickness.

Cut the dough into 1-inch wide strips, and roll each strip into a rope 1/2-inch thick. Cut the ropes into 9-inch lengths. Tie each dough rope in a loose knot, leaving one end short. Put on greased baking sheet. Pinch the short end to shape a head and beak. Poke a clove in the head for an eye. Flatten the other end for the tail. Snip end of tail twice. Let rise. Brush with beaten egg. Bake at 400 degrees for 15 minutes.

Corn Bread Diego Rivera

Serves 8

This is from LACMA's *Entertaining is an Art* cookbook.

2 eggs
1 cup corn cut from cob or from frozen corn kernels, defrosted
1 tablespoon baking powder
1 1/2 teaspoons salt
1 cup sour cream
2/3 cup melted butter
1 cup yellow cornmeal
14-ounce can peeled green chilies
1 cup finely diced Jack cheese, divided

Beat eggs and mix with all ingredients except chilies and cheese. Pour half of mixture into a greased 9-inch square pan. Place chilies on top of mixture. Cover with half of the cheese. Add remaining batter, and cover with remainder of cheese. Bake at 350 degrees for 45 minutes to an hour. Cut into squares and serve without butter.

Swedish Coffee Bread

Makes 2 loaves

Nana made this bread in her Berkeley apartment. I remember Marin and Anders awakening us with this delicacy on St. Lucia morning.

1 cup milk
1/2 cup shortening
3/4 cup sugar
1/2 teaspoon salt
3 cardamom seeds, crushed
1 egg
1 1 1/2 yeast packages
3-4 cups flour
confectioners' sugar
milk

Scald milk; add shortening, sugar, and salt. Cool to lukewarm. Remove pods from cardamom seeds, mash, and add to milk mixture. Beat egg and stir into cooled milk. Crumble yeast into mixture, stirring until dissolved. Add flour to form soft mixture. Turn onto a floured board and knead 20 minutes until smooth and elastic. Place in a greased bowl, smooth top with melted shortening, and allow to rise until doubled in bulk. Punch down and braid into two long strips. Place braids on cookie sheet in a warm place, allowing the bread to rise again until nearly doubled. Spread a thin paste of confectioner's sugar and milk on top. Bake at 375 degrees for 30 minutes.

Onion-Parmesan Puffs

Makes 2 dozen

From Lee Bailey's *Soup Meals*. The puffs enhance vegetable soups.

1 1/2 cups water
3/4 cups (1 1/2 sticks) unsalted butter, divided
2 cups coarsely chopped onions
2 teaspoons salt
1 1/2 cups all-purpose flour
6 eggs
1 cup freshly grated Parmesan cheese
milk
extra Parmesan cheese for top

Preheat oven to 400 degrees. Grease two cookie sheets. Bring water to boil in a medium saucepan and add 1/2 cup of butter. Meanwhile, sauté onions in remaining butter until wilted, about 5 minutes. Set aside.

When butter has melted and mixture is boiling again, add salt and flour. Turn heat down to low and stir for a few minutes until mixture pulls away from the sides of the pan. Remove from stove. Beat in eggs one at a time, mixing well after each addition. Combine cheese with dough and then the sautéed onions, mixing thoroughly. Drop heaping tablespoons of dough onto greased cookie sheets. Brush tops with milk and sprinkle with additional parmesan cheese. Bake about 35-40 minutes until golden and puffy.

Buttermilk Drop Biscuits

Makes 18

These are excellent with traditional dinners, such as a roast or meat loaf. This is an updated version of biscuits my grandmother Gaby made.

    2 cups all-purpose flour
    1 teaspoon salt
    2 teaspoons baking powder
    1/2 teaspoon baking soda
    6 tablespoons chilled unsalted butter
    1 1/2 cups buttermilk

Preheat oven to 450 degrees. Sift flour, salt, baking powder, and baking soda together into a large bowl. Cut butter into chunks and then cut into the flour with two knives until the butter is the size of large peas. Add the buttermilk all at once, stirring just enough to mix. Drop by tablespoons onto an ungreased cookie sheet, leaving a few inches between biscuits. Bake for 12–15 minutes until golden brown.

Cream Biscuits

Makes 1 dozen

Good with butter and jam or with ham and honey mustard.

  2 cups all-purpose flour
  1 tablespoon baking powder
  1 teaspoon salt
  5 1/2 tablespoons cold unsalted butter
  1 cup heavy cream, plus additional if necessary

Preheat oven to 425 degrees. Lightly grease a baking sheet. Sift flour, baking powder, and salt. Cut 5 tablespoons butter into bits, blending with flour until mixture resembles coarse meal. Add cream, stirring until just combined. Transfer to a floured surface and form into a ball. Roll into an 8 1/2-inch round. Cut out biscuits. Melt remaining 1/2 tablespoon butter and brush biscuit tops. Bake 1 inch apart on sheet until pale golden and cooked through, 15–20 minutes.

Sandwiches

Berkeley, California

*I had three chairs in my house; one for solitude,
two for friendship, three for society.*

—Henry David Thoreau

Hot Crab Salad Sandwiches

Serves 6–8

All of the crab lovers in our family have enjoyed these.

3 (6-ounce) cans lump crabmeat, drained
3 cups shredded Muenster cheese, divided
12 tablespoons chopped green onions, divided
6 tablespoons mayonnaise
3 teaspoons Worcestershire sauce
12 English muffins, split

Combine crabmeat, 1 1/2 cups cheese, 9 tablespoons green onions, mayonnaise, and Worcestershire sauce. Season with pepper.

Preheat broiler. Arrange muffin halves, split side up, on baking sheet. Broil just until beginning to color, about 1 minute. Mound 1/6 of crabmeat mixture on each muffin half. Top with remaining cheese and remaining green onions, dividing evenly. Broil until filling is heated through and cheese melted, about 2 minutes.

The Very Best Grilled Cheese Sandwiches

Serves 4

This recipe is from *Nancy Silverton's Sandwich Book: The Best Sandwiches Ever—from Thursday Nights at Campanile*. We celebrated Karl's receiving his doctorate at UCLA at this restaurant.

    8 slices white sour dough bread
    8 ounces Gruyère cheese, thinly sliced
    2-4 tomatoes, sliced 1/4 inch thick
    1-2 tablespoons extra virgin olive oil
    Kosher salt to taste

Set half the bread slices buttered side down. Cover with cheese. Drizzle olive oil over tomato slices. Sprinkle with salt; allow to sit 5 minutes. Place tomatoes on cheese slices. Place remaining bread on top, buttered side up. Grill. Cut sandwiches in half on diagonal.

Deviled Egg and Radish Sandwiches

Makes 8

If you like deviled eggs, you will enjoy these. The recipe came from the *San Francisco Chronicle*.

4 large eggs
2 tablespoons chopped radishes
1 1/2 tablespoons chopped green onions
3 tablespoons mayonnaise
1 tablespoon sour cream
2 teaspoons coarse-grained mustard
1/4 teaspoon pepper
1/2 teaspoon salt
8 thin slices wheat bread
butter
1 1/4 cups alfalfa sprouts

Mix all ingredients except butter and sprouts. Butter bread slices, and pile mixture on each piece evenly. Top with sprouts and serve open face.

Curry Ripe Olive Sandwiches

Serves 6

This recipe is from a North Carolina cookbook in the 1970's. Erik loves it.

    2 cups ripe black olives, chopped
    1 cup sliced green onions
    3 cups cheddar cheese
    1 cup mayonnaise
    1/2 teaspoon salt
    1 teaspoon curry powder
    6 English muffins

Mix all ingredients thoroughly except muffins. Split muffins and toast backs lightly. Pile mixture high on muffins and place under broiler until puffy and brown.

Greek Lamb Burgers with Spinach and Red Onion Salad

Serves 4

This recipe for a "modern burger" is from a 2008 food magazine.

1/2 cup chopped fresh mint
2 teaspoons paprika
3/4 teaspoon cinnamon
1/2 teaspoon salt
3 tablespoons olive oil, divided
1/2 pound ground lamb
4 hamburger buns
1 1/2 cups baby spinach leaves
1 1/3 cups feta cheese, crumbled
4 (1/4-inch thick) red onion slices
1 1/2 teaspoons balsamic vinegar

Mix mint, paprika, cinnamon, salt, and 1/2 tablespoon oil in a medium bowl. Mix in the lamb. Shape into four 3/4-inch thick patties. Cook in a nonstick skillet over medium-heat, 4 minutes per side for medium.

Preheat broiler. Broil buns until golden, 2 minutes. Top bun bottoms with burgers. Toss spinach, feta, onion, vinegar, and 1 1/2 tablespoons oil in a bowl. Place salad on top of burgers. Cover with the tops.

Tuna Salad with Dill and Capers I

Serves 8

This is an excellent tuna salad. Recipe is from the *San Francisco Chronicle*.

2 (6-ounce) cans tuna in brine or olive oil, well drained
2 bunches green onions
2 celery stalks, chopped
2-4 teaspoons capers
4-6 tablespoons mayonnaise
2 teaspoons brown mustard
1 teaspoon lemon juice or to taste
2 tablespoons extra virgin olive oil
2-4 tablespoons fresh dill
lettuce
salt and pepper to taste
16 slices whole grain bread

Mix tuna with a fork. Add green onions, celery, capers, mayonnaise, mustard, lemon juice, olive oil, and dill. Season with salt and pepper. Add lettuce.

Reuben Sandwiches

Serves 6

I received this recipe from my AOII housemother, Mrs. Guthrie.

18 slices Russian rye bread
1 1/4 cups Thousand Island dressing
12 slices Swiss cheese
1/2 cup sauerkraut, divided
1/2 cup corned beef
¼-1/2 cup softened butter

Spread bread with dressing. Arrange 1 cheese slice, 2 teaspoons sauerkraut and 2 slices corned beef on 12 slices. Stack bread slices to make 6 sandwiches. Cover with remaining bread slices and secure with toothpicks. Spread outside surfaces with softened butter and grill until cheese is melted and sandwich is heated through. Continue sequence with other sandwiches. Cut diagonally into 3 pieces.

Olive and Fennel Tuna Melt II

Serves 8

This unusual tuna sandwich is for you if you like olives.

    4 (6 1/2 ounce cans) solid white tuna, drained well
    2/3 cup mayonnaise
    3 1/3 cups finely chopped fennel
    10 Kalamata black olives, chopped
    2 tablespoons parsley leaves, minced
    2 tablespoons lemon juice
    8 slices rye bread, toasted
    8 ounces sharp cheddar cheese, grated

Preheat broiler. Flake tuna and stir in mayonnaise, fennel, olives, parsley, lemon juice, and salt and pepper. Divide tuna salad among toast slices topping with cheddar. In a shallow pan, broil sandwiches about 4 inches from heat until cheese is bubbling, 1-2 minutes.

Double Cheese Tortilla Stacks

Serves 6

I love this Mexican-Southwestern version of grilled cheese sandwiches.

9 ounces shredded Muenster cheese, divided
6 (9-inch) flour tortillas
6 tablespoons minced red onion, divided
6 tablespoons minced mild chilies, divided
9 ounces cheddar cheese, divided
Black pepper

Preheat oven to 450 degrees. Divide cheese among 3 tortillas, leaving half an inch bare around the edges. Sprinkle with 1 tablespoon onion and chili pepper. Cover with another tortilla. Top tortilla with cheddar and rest of onion and chili pepper. Sprinkle with black pepper. Top each stack with a third tortilla. Slide tortilla stacks onto baking sheet. Bake until edges are toasted and cheese melted, 10 minutes. Cool and cut each stack into 4 wedges. Serve 2 wedges per person.

Cucumber Watercress Tea Sandwiches

Serves 6

These are a delicious addition to a bridal or baby shower or art opening.

4 fresh cucumbers
4 tablespoons (1/2 stick) unsalted butter, at room temperature
8 thin slices white sandwich bread
1/2 cup watercress leaves, plus more
1/2 cup radish, onion, or sunflower sprouts
coarse salt to taste

Use paper towels to put cut surfaces of the cucumber slices to remove excess moisture. Lightly butter one side of each bread slice. Scatter watercress leaves evenly over all of the buttered bread. Layer cucumber slices over the watercress on four of the bread slices. Top the cucumber with the sprouts and a pinch of salt. Top with the remaining four bread slices, buttered side down.

Cut off crusts and slice sandwiches in half diagonally twice.
Arrange on one large platter. Garnish each sandwich with a watercress leaf.
Serve immediately.

Tillamook Toast

Serves 4

This recipe is from the Oregon Coast Aquarium's *Seafood Cookbook*. Bob and I visited Kris in Corvallis after his graduation from OSU and visited Newport.

4 (1-inch) thick slices French bread
olive oil
4 ounces Dungeness crab meat
1/4 cup mayonnaise
2 tablespoons lemon juice
1 tablespoon Worcestershire sauce
1/4 teaspoon dill
4 slices aged Tillamook cheddar cheese

Preheat broiler. Brush bread slices with olive oil. Place under broiler and toast until lightly browned. In a small bowl, mix crab, mayonnaise, lemon juice, Worcestershire sauce, and dill. Divide mixture on the toasts, topping with cheese. Melt cheese.

Soups

Berkeley, California

How marvelous it must be to spend the first ten or fifteen years of your life in the same place, and more marvelous still, to be able to return to that place of your childhood and see it through the eyes of a man.

—Harry Crews

Potato-Leek Soup in Bread Bowls

Serves 4

This soup is time consuming but unique. Bread loaves may be purchased.

1/2 teaspoon olive oil
1 medium onion, finely chopped
2 large leeks, thinly sliced
1 shallot, minced
2 large potatoes, peeled and finely diced
4 cups chicken broth
2 tablespoons finely diced fresh dill
salt and pepper to taste
4 unsliced round bread loaves
4 teaspoons olive oil
2 cloves garlic, crushed
3 tablespoons grated parmesan cheese
1/8 teaspoon nutmeg
chopped parsley for garnish

Heat 1/4 teaspoon oil in large pot over medium heat. Add onion, leeks and shallot. Cook, covered for 10-12 minutes or until tender, stirring occasionally. Add potatoes, broth, dill salt and pepper. Bring to a boil; reduce heat to low. Simmer, covered for 20 minutes or until potatoes are tender

Cut lids from bread leaving 3/4 inch edge. Hollow out centers. Remove bread to make croutons at a later time, if desired. Brush inside each loaf with 1 teaspoon oil. Rub insides with garlic; sprinkle with cheese. Place loaves and lids on baking sheet. Bake at 30 for 12-15 minutes or until cheese melts.

Strain soup through a sieve into another pot. Place solids in blender or food processor. Add a cup of the hot soup. Process until smooth. Whisk back into remaining soup to thicken. Stir in nutmeg. Cook until heated through. Spoon hot soup into bread bowls. Top with parsley.

Yellow-Pepper Gazpacho I

Serves 6

My mother introduced me to gazpacho. This recipe and the next are variations of her soup.

  6 yellow bell peppers, chopped
  2 hothouse cucumbers, chopped
  3/4 cup chopped red onions
  1 garlic clove, minced
  4 ripe tomatoes, chopped
  2 cups chicken stock
  1/4 cup white wine vinegar
  2 tablespoons capers, drained
  salt and pepper to taste

Place the vegetables in a large bowl. Add stock, vinegar, and capers. Season to taste with salt and pepper. Chill at least 3 hours.

Gazpacho II

Serves 6

This recipe is from one of my first cookbooks, bought in the early 1960's.

2 cups V-8 juice, divided
2 tablespoons olive oil
2 tablespoons red wine vinegar
1 chicken bouillon cube
1/2 teaspoon garlic salt
1/2 teaspoon salt
1/2 teaspoon pepper
1/2 teaspoon hot pepper sauce
1 ripe tomato, peeled and cubed
1 cup peeled diced cucumber
1/4 cup diced green pepper
1/4 cup diced onion
croutons and chopped tomatoes or cucumbers for garnish
3 dashes hot sauce

In food processor, combine 1 cup V-8 juice, oil, vinegar, bouillon cube, garlic salt, salt, pepper, and hot pepper sauce at medium speed for a few seconds. Add tomato, cucumber, green pepper, and onion. Process until tomato is evenly chopped, but not puréed. Add remaining 1 cup of juice. Pour into covered 1-quart container and chill overnight. Garnish with chopped vegetables, croutons, and hot sauce.

Cream of Green Chili Soup

Serves 6

Loved in New Mexico, this is from Santa Fe's Anasazi Restaurant.

1 1/2 cups chicken broth
1/2 cup minced onion
1 large garlic clove
1/2 pound mild green roasted chilies (Anaheim chilies)
8 ounces cream cheese
1 cup sour cream
1/4 teaspoon cumin
1 cup half and half
white pepper to taste
salt to taste

Bring broth to a boil with onion, for 5 minutes. Cool. In a food processor, chop garlic and chilies. Add cream cheese, sour cream, and cumin. With motor running, add broth mixture in a stream, and blend until well combined, Transfer to a bowl, and stir in half and half, white pepper, and salt. Cover soup, and chill overnight.

Apple Broccoli Soup

Serves 4

This soup is from *California Heritage Continues,* published in 1987.

    2 tablespoons butter
    1 small onion, thinly sliced
    1 large Golden Delicious apple, peeled, cored, and chopped
    3/4 pound broccoli
    2 cups chicken stock
    salt and white pepper to taste
    sour cream

Melt butter. Add onions and apple. Cover and cook until soft, 5–7 minutes. Chop broccoli, separating flowerets. Add stock and broccoli, bringing to a boil. Reduce heat, and simmer uncovered until tender. Purée. Reheat. Season to taste. Garnish with a dollop of sour cream.

Swiss Onion Soup

Serves 8–10

Bob and I first enjoyed onion soup in New York City in 1960. This recipe, from *City Cuisine* cookbook, is from the restaurant City.

    8 tablespoons (1 stick) unsalted butter
    3 medium onions, thinly sliced
    2 teaspoons salt
    1/4 teaspoon white pepper
    1/2 day-old French bread, diced
    1 teaspoon granulated sugar
    1/2 gallon whole milk
    1 pound Gruyère cheese, diced

Melt butter over moderate heat in a large Dutch oven. Cook onions with salt and pepper until soft, about 15 minutes. Add bread and sugar. Stir constantly for 1 minute. Add milk and bring to a boil. Add cheese. Stir and reduce to a simmer. Cook uncovered, stirring occasionally, 1 hour and 15 minutes. Serve immediately.

Black Bean Soup

Serves 4

Very easy! I first made this in Portland for Alexander and Erikson.

  2 tablespoons oil
  1 onion, diced into 1/2-inch pieces
  2 (15-ounce) cans black beans
  1 teaspoon cumin
  2 tablespoons chopped cilantro, divided
  1 1/2 cups water
  pepper, freshly ground
  Store bought corn chips

In a medium pot, heat 2 oil. Add the onion and cook over moderate heat until softened, about 6 minutes. Add the cumin and cook for 1 minute. Add the beans and their liquid and a 1 1/2 cups water. Bring to a simmer and cook until slightly thickened, about 15 minutes. Stir in 1 tablespoon of the cilantro and season with salt and pepper. Ladle the soup into bowls and top with a few broken chips. Sprinkle the remaining tablespoon of cilantro and serve.

Lazy Day Vegetable Soup

Serves 6

This has been a staple for our family from the 1970's. From a North Carolina Junior League cookbook, the soup may be made ahead.

1 1/2 pounds ground beef
1 onion, chopped
1 can cream of mushroom soup
1 can cream of celery soup
3 (12-ounce) cans V-8 juice
1 package frozen mixed vegetables
salt and pepper to taste

Brown ground beef and onion. Add remaining ingredients and cook until all vegetables are tender. Add salt and pepper to taste.

Red Cherry and Yellow Plum Tomato Soup

Serves 6

The presentation of this soup is beautiful, and I love making it.

4 baskets red cherry tomatoes
4 baskets yellow plum tomatoes
6 tablespoons chicken stock, divided
2 teaspoons white wine vinegar, divided
2 tablespoons olive oil, divided
pinch of sugar
salt and pepper to taste
crème fraiche for garnish

Cut cherry tomatoes in half and toss with 3 tablespoons chicken stock, 1 teaspoon vinegar, 1 tablespoon olive oil, pinch of sugar, and salt and pepper. Process in batches in a food processor. Strain.

Make another portion of soup using the remaining ingredients and the yellow plum tomatoes.

To serve, take two ladles and fill each one with one color soup, and pour the soups simultaneously into individual bowls. Place crème fraiche in a squeeze bottle and make a design on each serving.

Grape and Almond Gazpacho

Serves 12

This unique soup is from *Food & Wine* magazine. Members of my book group love it.

    2 pounds seedless green grapes
    1 small cucumber, peeled, seeded and coarsely chopped
    1/2 cup toasted almonds
    2 green onions, white and green parts, coarsely chopped
    1/4 cup rice vinegar
    1/2 cup plain yogurt
    3 ounces cream cheese
    2 tablespoons extra virgin olive oil
    1/4 cup buttermilk
    1/2-3/4 teaspoon salt
    1/2 teaspoon white pepper
    1/8-1/4 teaspoon cayenne pepper
    2 large dill sprigs, minced
    minced chives or sprigs of dill for garnish

Combine grapes, cucumber, almonds, green onions, vinegar, yogurt, cream cheese, olive oil, and buttermilk in a food processor or blender. Process until almost smooth, with just a bit of texture remaining. Stir in salt, white pepper, cayenne, and dill. Cover and refrigerate overnight. Serve in cold bowls and garnish with minced chives or dill. May be served in small cups to drink.

Tortilla Soup

Serves 8–10

This soup is from Chef Dionicia at Ernesto's Restaurant in Puerto Vallarta.

12 whole Roma tomatoes
3 teaspoons oregano (Mexican is best)
10 garlic cloves
5 bay leaves
6 large peppercorns
3 teaspoons small peppercorns
2 teaspoons marjoram
1 teaspoon thyme
1 tablespoon salt
3 1/2 quarts water, divided
1/4 cup onions
4 tablespoons chicken bouillon granules
5 chicken breasts, boned and skinned
8 corn tortillas, cut into thin slices
4 cups shredded mozzarella cheese

Boil tomatoes 10 minutes Place tomatoes and next 8 ingredients in blender, mixing for 4 minutes.

Sauté onion in oil and add blender contents by pouring through a strainer. Add 2 quarts water to strainer and swirl.

Put leftover ingredients from strainer in 1/2 cup water, blend well, and strain. Add another quart of water. Add chicken bouillon and chicken pieces, boiling until chicken is cooked.

Fry tortilla strips in oil until crispy.
Heat 10 ounces stock for each serving.

Fill each bowl with handful of tortilla strips, 3–4 avocado slices, and chicken breast slices. Cover with mozzarella cheese.

Pour boiling broth over ingredients in each bowl and serve.

Asparagus Soup

Serves 6

Asparagus is one of my favorite vegetables. This soup—from *Soup Meals* by Lee Bailey—was one of the first from this outstanding cookbook. I love serving a soup and salad for lunches. There are other delicious soups from this cookbook by Lee Bailey not included in my cookbook.

1 1/2 pounds asparagus, tough ends removed
1/4 cup (1/2 stick) unsalted butter
1/2 cup chopped onion
1 cup leeks, washed and chopped, white part only
1/2 cup chopped celery
1 small baking potato, peeled and cubed
3 1/2 cups chicken stock
1 teaspoon lemon juice
salt and white pepper to taste
paprika
1/2 cup half and half
crème fraiche or whipping cream for garnish

Snap off asparagus tips and set stalks aside. Melt butter in skillet with a cover. Add asparagus tips, onion, leeks, celery, and potato. Cover, and cook over lowest heat until vegetables are soft, 25 minutes.

Meanwhile, place chicken stock in a large pan with reserved asparagus stalks, cut into large pieces. Bring to a boil and simmer, covered, for 30 minutes. Discard stalks and set stock aside.

In a food processor, purée softened vegetables and add to asparagus stock. Season with lemon juice, salt, white pepper, and paprika. Allow to cool, and then refrigerate.

Stir in half and half. Serve with garnish of crème fraiche or whipped cream and pinch of paprika.

Chilled Tomatillo and Cucumber Soup

Serves 12

Erik and Laura provided this delicious soup from their outstanding recipe collection. I first tasted tomatillos in Berkeley in 1995 and love using them.

4 poblano chilies
2 tablespoons olive oil
1 pound tomatillos, husked, rinsed and cut into 1/2-inch pieces
2 English cucumbers, peeled and chopped
2 cups chopped onions
4 garlic cloves, minced
8 cups low-salt chicken broth
4 tablespoons seeded and minced jalapenos
4 tablespoons fresh lime juice
4 tablespoons chopped cilantro
1 cup whipping cream
salt and pepper to taste
4 green onions, chopped

Char poblano chilies over flame or under broiler until blackened on all sides. Enclose in paper bag; cool 10 minutes. Peel and seed chilies, then cut into 1-inch pieces.

Heat oil in heavy saucepan over medium heat. Add tomatillos, onion and cucumber; sautéing until onion begins to brown, about 5 minutes. Add broth and poblano chilies; bring to boil. Reduce heat to medium-low and simmer until tomatillos are tender, about 10 minutes. Stir in jalapenos, lime juice, and cilantro. Cool completely. Working in batches, purée soup in blender. Transfer to large bowl; stir in cream. Season to taste with salt and pepper. Chill overnight. Pour into glasses. Sprinkle with green onions and serve.

Cold Cucumber Soup

Serves 6

I love cucumber soup, and this recipe surpasses my favorite soup at Fullerton's Velvet Turtle.

4 cucumbers
2 quarts buttermilk, divided
1 quart sour cream
3/4 cup lemon juice
2 teaspoons salt
3 tablespoons dill weed
1/2 cup chopped parsley
8 scallions, sliced

Cut 12 thin slices from unpeeled cucumbers and reserve. Peel, seed, and chop the remainder of the cucumbers. Place half of the chopped cucumbers and 1 cup buttermilk in a food processor and blend until smooth. Pour into a large bowl. Place the other half of the chopped cucumbers and 1 cup buttermilk into the food processor. Add sour cream, lemon juice, salt, and dill weed, and blend until smooth. Add parsley and scallions and blend again until smooth.

Pour into the bowl with the first portion, and beat in the remaining buttermilk with a wire whisk. Chill. Garnish with the sliced cucumbers.

Butternut Squash Soup with Marsala and Thyme

Serves 8–10

From *Thanksgiving, Festive Recipes for the Holiday Table*, a Williams-Sonoma cookbook, this recipe has been on many of our Thanksgiving tables since we moved to Berkeley in 1995.

> 1 3-pound butternut squash, halved lengthwise, fibers and seeds removed
> 6 slices bacon, chopped
> 2 pounds yellow onions, chopped
> 1/2 tablespoons chopped fresh thyme
> 5 1/4 cups chicken broth
> 1/3 cup cream or half and half
> 3 tablespoons dry Marsala wine
> pinch of cayenne
> salt and pepper
> fresh thyme leaves for garnish

Preheat oven to 375 degrees. In a baking pan, place squash cut sides down. Add water to pan to a depth of 1/2 inch. Bake until squash is tender, 50 minutes. Remove from oven and cool. Using a spoon, scrape the flesh from the skin. You will need 3 3/4 cups for the soup.

In a large, heavy saucepan over medium heat, sauté bacon until fat is rendered, 3 minutes. Add onions and chopped thyme, sautéing until tender, about 8 minutes. Remove from heat.

Transfer onion mixture to a food processor. In two or more batches, add the squash and purée until smooth. Return the purée to saucepan. Place over medium-low heat and mix in the 5 1/4 cups broth. Simmer uncovered, stirring occasionally for 20 minutes to blend the flavors. Stir in the cream or half and half and the Marsala. Add the cayenne and season to taste with salt and pepper. If the soup is too thick, thin with additional stock to desired consistency.

Ladle into individual bowls. Garnish with thyme leaves. Serve hot.

Sorrel Soup

Serves 6

There are many recipes for sorrel soup. This is my favorite. I have served it with cheese wafers (See Breads). Both recipes are from Lee Bailey's *Soup Meals*.

    3 tablespoons unsalted butter
    1 pound yellow onions, coarsely chopped
    1 garlic clove, minced
    5 cups chicken stock
    salt and pepper to taste
    1 pound red potatoes, peeled and coarsely chopped
    12 ounces sorrel leaves, trimmed and torn into large pieces
    sour cream

Heat butter in a deep pot. When melted add onions and saute until wilted and turning golden, about 5 minutes. Add garlic and cook for another minute. Add stock and heat. Add potatoes. Simmer until potatoes are done, about 10 minutes. Stir in sorrel and heat thoroughly. Transfer mixture to a food processor and puree. Return to the heat and cook for another few minutes, correcting seasoning with salt and pepper if necessary. Serve with a dollop of sour cream on top of each.

Cream of Lettuce Soup

Serves 6

An unusual soup from the 1989 *City Cuisine* cookbook by Susan Feninger and Mary Sue Milliken. We enjoyed the authors/chefs terrific Los Angeles restaurants City and Border Grill with Karl.

2 tablespoons unsalted butter
1 1/2 medium onions, sliced
1 slice bacon
1 1/2 teaspoons salt
1/2 teaspoon white pepper
1 red potato, peeled and sliced
4 cups chicken stock
1 large head Bibb lettuce, leaves separated, washed and chopped
1 cup heavy cream
1 cup half & half

Melt butter over medium heat in a large Dutch oven. Cook onions with bacon, salt, and pepper until soft, about 10 minutes. Add potato and chicken stock. Bring to a boil.

Reduce heat to a simmer and cook uncovered, about 15 minutes. Remove and discard bacon. Return stock to a boil; reduce to a simmer and stir in lettuce. Cook over moderate heat uncovered, 3-4 minutes. Puree in a blender until smooth. Strain into a pot, extracting all juices by pressing down with a ladle. Stir in cream and half & half. Bring to a boil and then remove from heat.

Minted Pea Soup

Serves 4

A good use of mint from your garden.

    3 tablespoons vegetable oil
    2 cups finely chopped white onions
    1 (10-ounce) box frozen spinach, thawed
    4 cups chicken stock
    3 (10-ounce) boxes frozen peas, thawed
    1 small bunch fresh mint leaves, stems removed
    1/2 cup buttermilk
    1/2 cup heavy cream
    salt and black pepper to taste
    1 carrot, shredded
    1/3 cup chopped mint leaves

Heat oil in a large pan. Add the onions and cook over high heat until soft. Squeeze out excess water from the spinach and add to the onions. Add the peas and stock. Bring to a boil and continue to simmer, 10 minutes. Add mint leaves. Pour half the mixture into a food processor, reserving 1/2 cup liquid. Process and set aside.

Mix the remaining mixture in the processor. Add to the first mixture and stir in the buttermilk and cream. Add reserved liquid until the desired consistency is reached. Refrigerate for 1 hour and serve chilled. Add shredded carrots and exra mint leaves for grnish.

Salads

San Leandro, California

We shape our dwellings, and then our dwellings shape us.

—Winston Churchill

Watermelon & Avocado Salad I

Serves 4

I first saw this recipe in the *San Francisco Chronicle* in spring 2007.

3 tablespoons raspberry vinegar
3 tablespoons extra virgin olive oil
Kosher salt and pepper to taste
2 avocados, ripe but firm
juice from 1 lemon
4 ounces mixed salad greens
3 cups diced seedless watermelon
4 ounces feta cheese, crumbled
2 teaspoons chopped chives
1 tablespoon julienned basil
1/4 cup pine nuts, toasted (optional)

Whisk together the vinegar and oil in a small bowl. Season with salt and pepper. Just before serving, cut the avocados into small cubes. Set aside, sprinkling with lemon to prevent discoloration. Toss enough of the vinaigrette, about 1 tablespoon, with the salad greens to just moisten the leaves. Divide greens onto chilled plates. Top with avocado and watermelon. Drizzle with the rest of the vinaigrette. Garnish with feta cheese, herbs, pine nuts (if using) and an additional sprinkle of salt and grind of pepper.

Watermelon Salad with Feta and Mint II

Serves 12

This recipe was in *Food & Wine* and was created by Chef Jacques Pepin.

1/2 cup extra virgin olive oil
3 tablespoons fresh lemon juice
1/2 pound or 2 cups feta cheese, crumbled
1 1/4 cups coarsely chopped Kalamata olives
1 small sweet onion, diced into 1/2-inch pieces
2 teaspoons kosher salt
1 teaspoon Tabasco sauce
1/2 teaspoon pepper, freshly ground
1 (8-pound) seedless watermelon, cubed into 1/2-inch pieces
mint, for garnish

Whisk oil, lemon juice, feta, Kalamata olives, and onion. Add water-melon. Toss gently, and garnish with mint.

Mixed Cherry Tomatoes with Tamarind Dressing

Serves 6

This easy and unique salad recipe also came from *Food & Wine.*

1/2 teaspoon cumin seeds
1/2 teaspoon fennel seeds
2 teaspoons tamarind concentrate or balsamic vinegar
2 tablespoons hot water
2 tablespoons honey
1 tablespoon olive oil
1/4 teaspoon salt
1/4 teaspoon pepper
3 cups cherry tomatoes

Toast cumin and fennel seeds; then coarsely crush using a mortar and pestle. If using tamarind concentrate whisk into hot water until dissolved. Whisk in honey, oil, salt and pepper until blended. Add tomatoes and spices, tossing to coast. Let stand at room temperature for 1 hour. Season with additional salt if needed.

Red Potato Salad I

The first potato salad I made was in 1959 for a picnic at Stinson Beach with John and Sue Robbins. Bob and I were married a few months later. John was one of Bob's ushers. I phoned my mother asking for a recipe. This may or may not be the one she suggested.

2 1/2 pounds small red potatoes
salt
1 tablespoon lemon juice
1/2 cup sour cream
1/2 cup mayonnaise
1/4 cup fresh basil, cut into strips
1/4 cup minced parsley, no stems
1/2 teaspoon Dijon mustard
1/4 teaspoon ground pepper
1 garlic clove, minced
2 tablespoons vinegar
1 teaspoon Worcestershire sauce
1/2 teaspoon salt

Cover the potatoes with lightly salted water and add lemon juice. Bring to a rapid boil; turn heat down to just a rolling boil. Cook potatoes until tender when pierced with the point of a knife, about 12 minutes or more. Drain and cool. Meanwhile, whisk together all other ingredients to make a dressing. Cut cooled potatoes into small chunks, leaving the skins on, and toss with the dressing. Refrigerate until time to serve.

Classic Potato Salad II

Serves 6

Bob's sister Betty joined us for a 2012 Fourth of July lunch. I am not a lover of potato salad, but this one is the best! The recipe was from a *San Francisco Chronicle* writer who said, "The secret is dousing the warm cooked potatoes with vinegar and oil."

3 pounds red-skinned potatoes
1/4 cup wine vinegar
1/2 teaspoon kosher salt
4 tablespoons fruity olive oil, divided
1/2 cup mayonnaise, or more if desired for creaminess
1/2 cup minced Italian parsley
2 green onions, minced
1/2 cup minced sweet onions
1/2 cup ripe olives, pitted and halved

Cover potatoes with cold water. Bring to a boil, then reduce to a simmer and cook for 30–40 minutes. Test for tenderness with a thin paring knife. When cool enough to handle, peel, if desired, and cut into small chunks.

Meanwhile, whisk together the wine vinegar, salt, and 2 tablespoons of the olive oil. Pour over the warm potatoes, and let marinate at room temperature for about 1 hour. (This step makes all the difference between good and great.)

Just before serving, combine the remaining 2 tablespoons olive oil and the mayonnaise. Fold into the potatoes, along with the parsley, green onions, onion, and olives. Taste for seasoning. This potato salad is best served soon after making it, rather than allowing it to chill in the refrigerator for hours.

Tostada Compuesta

Serves 4

This recipe is similar to the one served at Estrada's Spanish Kitchen in Visalia. I love this salad and have eaten hundreds of them at Estrada's in both Fresno and Visalia. Unfortunately, the restaurants have closed.

   2 heads iceberg lettuce, shredded
   12 small crisp tortillas (Guerero brand)
   2 cans refried beans, thinned slightly with water
   El Pato hot sauce

Heat beans on stove. Preheat oven to 400 degrees. Place tortillas on a large baking sheet and heat. Cover with enough heated beans to cover the tortillas. Heat. Place shredded lettuce on top and heat a bit longer to just wilt lettuce.

Place 3 of the tortillas with beans and lettuce on each plate. Sprinkle about 3 teaspoons hot sauce on lettuce. Put on about 1/8 cup of cider vinegar dressing on top of the lettuce. Enjoy! (Dressing recipe is on next page.)

Apple Cider Vinegar Recipe for Tostada Compuesta

1 cup canola oil
1 cup apple cider vinegar
2 tablespoons honey
1/2 teaspoon sea salt
2 teaspoons garlic powder
pinch of pepper
1/2 teaspoon dried parsley

Add all ingredients to a blender and blend for 30 seconds. Put dressing into container.

Sugar Snap Pea and Cantaloupe Salad

Serves 6–8

This salad recipe from *California Cooking* is a wonderful beginning to a spring meal.

Salad

3/4 pound sugar snap peas, strings removed, slivered, and cut
1 cantaloupe, peeled, seeded, cut into slices 1/2-inch x 2-inches
1 1/2 bunches watercress, stems removed
2 teaspoons almonds, toasted for garnish

Sherry Vinaigrette Dressing

1 egg
2 tablespoons juice from fresh lemon
1/2 teaspoon dried tarragon, crushed
1 garlic clove, crushed
1/4 teaspoon salt
1/2 teaspoon anchovy paste
ground pepper, to taste
2 tablespoons red wine vinegar
1 tablespoon sherry
1 1/2 cups vegetable oil

Blanch sugar snap peas in boiling salted water for about 1 minute, until barely tender. Rinse immediately in cold water and dry well. In a small bowl combine all the vinaigrette ingredients except oil. Whisking constantly, add the oil slowly until well blended. To serve, spoon some of the vinaigrette onto individual salad plates, and arrange the snap peas, cantaloupe, and watercress on top. Drizzle with additional vinaigrette, and garnish with toasted slivered almonds.

Parsley Salad

Serves 6

Gustav Anders was my favorite Orange County restaurant. We dined here often for dinner and lunch. It closed in 2005. I always ordered this unusual Scandinavian salad.

Dressing

1/2 packed cup basil leaves
3/4 cup extra virgin olive oil
1/4 cup rice vinegar
salt and pepper to taste
1 shallot, minced
1 clove garlic, minced

Carefully wash basil to remove any sand, then dry well. Place the basil leaves in the bowl of a food processor; add oil, vinegar, and salt and pepper to taste; process until smooth. Stir shallots and garlic into the dressing.

Salad

4 packed cups curly parsley leaves
3 ounces coarsely grated or shaved Parmesan cheese
1 1/2 cups oil-packaged sundried tomatoes, drained and julienned
1 teaspoon minced garlic

Carefully wash parsley. Dry well and place in a salad bowl. Add cheese to the parsley. Add sun-dried tomatoes, along with the garlic. Toss well to combine. Drizzle dressing over salad and toss well to combine ingredients. Taste and adjust seasonings. Divide among salad plates, garnish with some shaved cheese, and serve.

Cranberry, Raspberry, Pear, and Orange Relish

Makes 4 cups

I don't have a special category for relishes. I serve this at Thanksgiving. It is from the Williams-Sonoma cookbook *Thanksgiving, Festive Recipes for the Holiday Table*.

> 1 thin-skinned orange, cut into 8 wedges, divided
> 1 (12-ounce) bag cranberries, divided
> 3/4 cup sugar, divided
> 1/2 teaspoon ground cardamom
> 2 firm pears, peeled, quartered and finely chopped

Cut orange wedges in half crosswise. Combine half of orange pieces, cranberries, and sugar in food processor. Mix until finely chopped. Transfer mixture to a bowl. Repeat with remaining oranges, cranberries, and sugar. Add to bowl. Add cardamom and pears to mixture and stir well. Taste and add more sugar, if desired. Cover and refrigerate until ready to serve.

Snow Pea Salad

Serves 6

This is a recipe that appeared in the *San Francisco Chronicle* Food Section in 2005.

Salad

1/4 pound bacon
1/4 pound snow peas
2 pounds frozen baby peas, thawed
1 small red onion, diced into 4-inch pieces
1/8 pound jicama, cut in 1/4-inch slices

Dressing

1/3 cup mayonnaise
1/3 cup sour cream
1/4 teaspoon nutmeg
pepper to taste
1/8 teaspoon kosher salt
1/8 teaspoon fresh mint, minced

Note: Peas should be thawed in refrigerator. To remove excess moisture, place thawed peas on paper towel. Let stand at room temperature 20–30 minutes.

Chop bacon in strips 1/4-inch wide and fry until crisp. Drain. Combine snow peas, baby peas, red onion, bacon, and jicama in bowl. In separate bowl, blend together mayonnaise, sour cream, nutmeg, pepper, salt, and mint. Pour over pea mixture and toss.

Baked Goat Cheese with Greens

Serves 4

This mouth-watering salad is offered at Chez Panisse Cafe, one I order every time I lunch there.

1/2 cup olive oil
4 fresh thyme sprigs
1 bay leaf, crumbled
2 (4-ounce) mild unflavored goat cheese logs
3 tablespoons balsamic vinegar
8 cups assorted baby greens (red leaf)
1 cup breadcrumbs, toasted
salt and pepper

Combine olive oil, thyme and bay leaf in a small bowl. Cut goat cheese logs into 4 1/2 inch rounds. Arrange in single layer in glass baking dish. Pour oil mixture over cheese, turning to coat. Cover and refrigerate overnight. Preheat oven to 450 degrees. Lightly oil baking sheet. Place breadcrumbs in bowl. Remove cheese from oil. Reserve oil. Coat each round with crumbs, pressing gently to adhere. Arrange cheese on baking sheet. Bake until lightly bubbling and golden, about 5 minutes.

While cheese is baking, whisk vinegar into reserved oil mixture and season with salt and pepper. Place greens in bowl. Pour over enough vinaigrette to coat lightly. Season with salt and pepper. Distribute on individual salad plates and top each with two hot cheese rounds.

Clementine Jicama Salad

Serves 8

I made this alternative to a green salad for Thanksgiving in 2014.

1/2 teaspoon chopped garlic
1/2 teaspoon salt
1/2 cup fresh lime juice
6 tablespoons olive oil
1/2 teaspoon sugar
1/2 teaspoon pepper
8 clementine oranges, peeled and cut into 1/4-inch slices
1 pound jicama, peeled and cut into 1/4-inch sticks, about 3 cups
1 small red onion, thinly sliced
1 cup cilantro sprigs
1/4 cup crumbled mild feta
1/3 cup toasted pumpkin seeds

Mince and mash garlic to a paste with 1/2 teaspoon salt; whisk with lime juice, oil, sugar, and 1/2 teaspoon pepper in a bowl. Before serving, add clementine oranges, jicama, onion, and cilantro. Toss. Season with salt. Sprinkle with crumbled feta cheese and pumpkin seeds. (Dressing may be made ahead and kept at room temperature.) Clementine oranges, jicama, and onion may be cut 4 hours ahead. Chill.

Corn Salad

Serves 6

Joyce Goldstein, author of *Casual Entertaining*, was the owner-chef of Square One in San Francisco, location of Erik and Laura's rehearsal dinner.

    6 ears corn (about 3 cups kernels)
    1/2 cup olive oil, divided
    1 cup minced red onion
    2 teaspoons chili powder
    1 teaspoon ground cumin
    1 red pepper, seeded and cut into 1/4-inch pieces
    1 green pepper, seeded and cut into 1/4-inch pieces
    1-1 1/2 cups seeded and diced tomatoes
    4 tablespoons chopped cilantro
    3 tablespoons sherry vinegar
    salt and pepper to taste

Shuck corn and cut off kernels. Bring a saucepan 3/4 full of salted water to a boil. Add corn kernels and boil for 1–3 minutes. Drain and immerse in cold water. Drain again and pat dry with paper towels.

In a small pan, warm 1/4 cup of olive oil. Add the onion and sauté for a few minutes, just to take the sharp bite out. Add the chili powder and cumin, and sauté for 1 minute longer.

In a serving bowl, combine the corn, red and green peppers, tomatoes, and cooled onions. Toss to mix. Add the cilantro, the remaining 1/4 cup olive oil, and the vinegar. Toss well to combine. Season to taste with salt and pepper. Toss again and serve.

Ritzy Ramen Salad

Serves 8

This *California Sizzles* salad is a favorite at book group and Art Guild luncheons.

Salad

    1 head cabbage, shredded
    6 green onions, sliced
    2 seasoning packets ramen soup mix, oriental flavor
    1/2 cup slivered almonds, lightly toasted
    1/2 cup sunflower seeds
    1 bunch chopped cilantro
    6 boned chicken breast halves, cooked and cut into bite-sized pieces

Dressing

    3/4 cup vegetable oil
    1/2 teaspoon salt
    6 tablespoons rice wine vinegar
    1/2 teaspoon pepper
    4 teaspoons sugar
    1 seasoning packet from one of the above ramen packages

Combine cabbage and green onions in large bowl and set aside. (May be done the night before serving.) Mix dressing ingredients and refrigerate. Just before serving, crumble uncooked soup noodles. Toss cabbage and onions with dressing and add almonds, sunflower seeds, cilantro, chicken, and noodles from the 2 ramen packages.

Chicken-Fruit Salad

Serves 6

This recipe from *Sunset* introduced me to capers. I first made it in 1965 in San Jose. Nana visited and was my guest at a mother-daughter church dinner.

    2 whole chicken breasts, cooked and diced
    1 cup celery, chopped
    2 tablespoons chopped green onions
    2 tablespoons chopped capers
    1 teaspoon salt
    2 tablespoons lemon juice
    4–5 cups red leaf and butter lettuce, torn
    1/2 cup mayonnaise
    1/2 teaspoon grated lemon peel
    1 (22-ounce) can mandarin oranges, drained
    1/2 cup toasted slivered almonds

Bake chicken: seasoned with 1 teaspoon salt, several peppercorns, and 1 small onion, until tender, about 30 minutes. Cool.

Combine chicken with celery, green onion and capers. Add salt and lemon juice. Cover and chill for several hours. Just before serving, add oranges (reserve a few for garnish), pineapple, and almonds. Combine mayonnaise and lemon peel; mix in carefully so as not to break fruit pieces. Spoon into a bowl lined with greens. (Double for a group.)

Brown Derby Cobb Salad

Serves 6

Bob and I enjoyed this salad at a Brown Derby restaurant on Wilshire Boulevard in Los Angeles and at Fullerton's Dal Rae.

Dressing

1/4 cup water
1/2 cup red wine vinegar
1/4 teaspoon sugar
1 1/2 teaspoons lemon juice
1/2 teaspoon salt
1/2 teaspoon pepper
1/2 teaspoon Worcestershire sauce
3/4 teaspoon English mustard
1/2 clove garlic, minced
3/4 cup vegetable oil
1/2 cup olive oil

Combine water, vinegar, sugar, lemon juice, salt, pepper, Worcestershire sauce, mustard, garlic, and both oils. Chill. Shake well before serving. Makes about 1 1/2 cups.

Salad

1/2 head Bibb lettuce
1/2 bunch watercress
1 small bunch chicory
1/2 head romaine
2 tablespoons minced chives
2 medium tomatoes, diced
2 chicken breasts, boned and diced

6 strips bacon, cooked and crumbled
1 avocado
3 hard-boiled eggs, chopped
1/2 cup crumbled Roquefort cheese

Chop lettuce, watercress, chicory, and romaine into fine pieces. Combine in a wide shallow bowl. Add chives. Peel, seed, and dice tomatoes. Dice chicken breasts, bacon, avocado, and eggs. Arrange ingredients in narrow strips across top of greens. Sprinkle with cheese. Chill. Toss with 1/2 cup French dressing.

Simply Caesar Salad

Serves 4

I have made this Caesar salad at least one hundred times through the years. I always remember my mother making marvelous croutons for her Caesar salad.

Salad

1 head Romaine lettuce
2 tablespoons olive oil
1 clove garlic, minced
1 1/2 cups Sourdough bread, cubed

Dressing

1/2 cup grated Parmesan cheese
1/4 cup olive oil
1/4 cup vegetable oil
1/4 cup lemon juice
2 cloves garlic, minced
1 teaspoon Worcestershire sauce

Combine all dressing ingredients in blender, mixing until smooth. Cover and refrigerate until ready to use, up to 2 days ahead. Rinse and tear lettuce into bite-sized pieces. Place in a bowl and chill.

Sauté bread in the oil and garlic until golden brown. When ready to serve, combine lettuce and desired amount of dressing. Top with garlic croutons.

Lime and Cilantro Chicken Salad

Serves 6

I enjoyed this salad with Toni at Nordstrom's in Portland in 2009.

Vinaigrette

1/2 cup rice wine vinegar
1/4 cup fresh lime juice
1 clove garlic, minced
2 teaspoons chipotle chilies in adobe sauce, puréed (they come canned
packed in adobe sauce.)
2 tablespoons honey
1/2 teaspoon sea salt
3/4 cup olive oil
1 cup chopped fresh cilantro

Salad

3 ears fresh corn, shucked and boiled
3-4 boneless, skinless chicken breasts, seasoned with salt and pepper,
cooked and julienned
1/2 cup diced cherry or grape tomatoes
3/4 cup roasted, salted green pumpkin seeds (also called "pepitas"}
1 pound mixed baby greens and arugula
1 cup grated Monterey jack cheese
1/2 cup chopped roasted red pepper
1/2 teaspoon kosher or sea salt
freshly ground black pepper
cilantro sprigs for garnish
lime wedges for garnish

For Vinaigrette

In a blender or food processor, combine vinegar, lime juice, garlic, puréed chipotle chilies, honey, and salt and process until thoroughly combined and smooth. With machine running, gradually add the oil in a thin, steady stream to form an emulsion. Add cilantro, and process to combine. Taste and adjust seasoning. Set aside.

For Salad

To assemble salad, cut off corn kernels from cobs. Add chicken, tomatoes, greens, Jack cheese, bell pepper and pumpkin seeds to the corn. Drizzle the vinaigrette over the salad. Toss gently to coat all the ingredients. Season to taste with salt and pepper. Garnish with cilantro sprigs and lime wedges. Serve.

Bleu Cheese Salad

Serves 6–8

The authors of Pasadena Jr. League's *California Sizzles* say, "Bleu cheese lovers will line up."

Salad

> 1 head cabbage, shredded
> 1/2 pound Bleu cheese, crumbled

Dressing

> 1/3 cup cider vinegar
> 1/4 teaspoon dry mustard
> 1 teaspoon celery seed
> 2 tablespoons sugar
> 2 cloves garlic, minced
> 1/4 cup minced onion
> salt and pepper to taste
> 1/4 cup vegetable oil

Mix cabbage and Bleu cheese. Combine all ingredients for dressing and whisk together. Add to salad.

Golden Triangle Cauliflower Salad

Serves 6

Karl and his close friend Doris served this salad. Doris was head of UCLA's poetry program and her husband Darryl was Art Department Chair at CSUF during the years I was active with Art Alliance and its docent program. Doris was his "Southern California mother."

1 tablespoon sesame seeds
1 1/2 heads cauliflower
1 tablespoon vinegar
1 teaspoon sugar, divided
1/4 teaspoon turmeric
salt
1/2 onion, thinly sliced
2-3 cloves garlic, minced
1/4 cup canola oil
1 teaspoon cumin
1 teaspoon coriander
1 teaspoon cardamom
1 teaspoon black mustard seeds
1 teaspoon paprika
juice of 1/2 lemon
salt to taste

Toast sesame seeds over medium heat until brown. Set aside.

Break up cauliflower heads into bite-sized florets. Place in a saucepan. Add water to cover. Add vinegar, 1/2 teaspoon sugar, turmeric, and salt to taste. Bring to a boil. Cover and simmer until cauliflower is tender. Drain and set aside.

Fry onion and garlic in oil to cover until golden brown and crisp. Drain and set aside.

Heat oil. Add cumin, coriander, cardamom, mustard seeds and paprika, stirring to blend. Add simmered cauliflower, remaining 1/2 teaspoon sugar, and lemon juice; stir until ingredients are combined and cauliflower is heated through. Season to taste with salt. Add fried onion, garlic, and toasted sesame seeds. Toss.

Avocado, Onion, Tomato and Hot Pepper Salad

Serves 6

From a Lee Bailey cookbook, this is similar to my mother's recipe.

3 tablespoons fresh lemon juice
6 tablespoons olive oil
salt and pepper
1 tablespoon minced cilantro
3 cups tomatoes, peeled, seeded and chopped
1 red onion, chopped
1 avocado, pitted and coarsely chopped
1 teaspoon mixed jalapeno

Whisk lemon juice, olive oil, salt, pepper, and cilantro. Set aside. Combine the other ingredients and toss with the vinaigrette. Serve with a slotted spoon in small bowls, as salad can be rather liquid.

Three Pea Salad

Serves 6

Eating this salad reminds me of shelling fresh peas with Nana in our Rodney Drive home in San Leandro when I was in kindergarten.

1 tablespoon shallots
1 teaspoon sherry vinegar
1 tablespoon sour cream or crème fraiche
1/4 cup extra-virgin olive oil
salt and freshly ground pepper
1/2 pound sugar snap peas
1/2 pound snow peas, halved crosswise
1 (10-ounce) box frozen baby peas

Bring salted water to boil. Fill a bowl with ice water. In another large bowl, whisk the shallots, vinegar, and sour cream together. Whisk in the olive oil until emulsified. Season with salt and pepper.

Add sugar snap peas to boiling water. Blanch for 20 seconds. Add snow peas and cook for 20 seconds longer, until sugar snap peas and snow peas are crisp. Add the frozen baby peas until they are just heated through. Drain all of the peas in a colander and immediately transfer to the ice water to stop the cooking. Drain again, and pat the peas dry. Add the peas to the dressing. Season with salt and pepper and toss to coat. Serve. The salad may be refrigerated overnight.

Frisée Salad with Poached Egg

Serves 6

Bob believed Karl was an outstanding cook, and if he had not been an English professor, he might have been a chef.

Salad

> 1 head mache lettuce, torn into pieces
> 1 tablespoon chopped parsley, tarragon, or chives
> 1 sweet red pepper, very thinly sliced
> 6 large eggs
> 1 tablespoon red wine vinegar
> salt to taste
> pepper to taste
> 1 teaspoon fresh thyme leaves for garnish

Dressing

> 2 tablespoons sherry, champagne, or red wine vinegar
> salt to taste
> 1 teaspoon Dijon mustard
> 1 small garlic clove, minced
> 1/3 cup extra virgin olive oil

Combine lettuce, herbs, and red pepper.

Poach eggs. Fill a lidded frying pan with water, and bring to a boil. Add 1 tablespoon vinegar to the water. One at a time, break the eggs into a teacup, then tip from the teacup into the pan (do this in batches if necessary). Immediately turn off the heat under the pan and cover tightly. Leave for 4 minutes. Lay a clean dishtowel next to the pan, and using a slotted spoon or spatula, carefully remove the poached eggs from the water. Set on the towel to drain.

Whisk together vinegars, salt, mustard, and garlic. Whisk in the oil. Toss with salad until thoroughly coasted, and distribute among the salad plates. Top each serving with a poached egg. Season the egg with salt and pepper to taste. Sprinkle with thyme leaves and serve.

Poultry

Fresno, California

"Home—the nursery of the infinite."

—William Ellery Channing

Chicken or Meat Filled Crepes

Serves 4–5

This recipe is an excellent use of leftover chicken or meat.

Crèpes

4 eggs
1/2 cup milk
1/2 cup water
2 tablespoons butter, melted
1 cup flour
3/4 teaspoon salt

Filling

1 onion, chopped
1 tablespoon butter
2 cups chopped meat or chicken
1/4 cup pimiento, chopped
salt and pepper to taste
stock to moisten
1 cup cheddar cheese for garnish
1/4 cup almonds, slivered and toasted

For Crepes

Beat ingredients. Let stand for 1 hour. Heat an 8-inch skillet. Brush with butter. Pour batter into pan by scant 1/4 cup. Turn and tip pan. Turn crèpes after a few seconds. Remove from pan.

For Filling

Sauté onion in butter. Mix with chopped meat or chicken, pimiento, salt, and pepper and a small amount of stock to moisten. Fill crèpes and roll up. Bake, topped with garnish of cheese and almonds, at 400 degrees for 10 minutes or until cheese is brown and bubbly.

Baked Chicken Cheddar

Serves 4

A 1970 Fullerton Assistance League cookbook was the source of this easy and delicious recipe.

4 boneless chicken breasts, diced
1 pint sour cream
1 (16-ounce) box cheese crackers, broken into crumbs
1/4 pound (1 cube) butter

Preheat oven to 350 degrees. Dip or spread chicken pieces with sour cream. Roll in cracker crumbs. Melt butter and put in a shallow baking dish. Lay chicken pieces in butter and turn, buttered side up. Bake 1–1 1/2 hours or until chicken is tender and golden brown.

Viva La Chicken Tortilla Casserole

Serves 8–10

This recipe is from a 1968 Fullerton cookbook. Our boys loved it.

4 whole boneless chicken breasts
1 dozen corn tortillas
1 (10 1/2-ounce) can cream of mushroom soup
1 (10 1/2-ounce) can cream of chicken soup
1 cup milk
1 onion, grated
1 (7-ounce) can green chile sauce
1 pound cheddar cheese, grated
2 teaspoons chicken stock or chicken broth

Wrap chicken breasts in foil and bake at 400 degrees for 1 hour. When cool, cut chicken into large pieces. Cut tortillas into 1-inch strips or quarters. Mix soups, milk, onion, and chile sauce. Grease a 9 x 13-inch shallow baking dish. Place about 2 tablespoons of broth in bottom of dish, then a layer of tortillas. Place a layer of chicken, then soup mixture. Repeat layers until all ingredients are used. End with soup mixture. Top with cheese. Cover and refrigerate. Bake at 300 degrees for 1 1/2 hours.

Tantalizing Turmeric Chicken

Serves 4

My AOII sorority "little sister" Gerry Martin Soderberg is a contributor to *California Sizzles*. When we moved back to California from Maryland in 1974, we had dinner at Gerry and Arnold's San Marino home. Kris enjoyed their pool. Perhaps this outing contributed to Kris learning to swim, joining a YMCA swimming team in Fullerton three years later, and in ninth grade, becoming a member of Sonora's swimming and water polo teams.

    4 chicken breasts, skinned and boned
    salt and pepper to taste
    1 tablespoon soy sauce
    1 1/2 teaspoons honey
    2 tablespoons fresh lemon juice
    1 tablespoon cumin
    1/2 teaspoon cayenne
    1 tablespoon ground cumin
    1/2 teaspoon turmeric
    2 teaspoons finely chopped garlic
    2 tablespoons olive oil

Place chicken in a mixing bowl. Add all ingredients, blending well so that the pieces are well coated. Cover with plastic wrap and refrigerate for 20 minutes to overnight. When ready to cook, heat oil in a skillet large enough to hold pieces without crowding. Over medium-high heat, add chicken and cook until browned on one side. Turn and reduce heat to medium. Cook until done, 10–15 minutes. Serve hot.

Sautéed Chicken with Olives, Capers & Roasted Lemons

Serves 4

This is from the chef/owner Lidia Bastianich's restaurant Lidia's in Kansas City. Bob and I dined here on an Art Guild trip. I first made this chicken entrée in Portland for Kris and Toni.

1/2 cup extra virgin olive oil, divided
2 lemons, sliced 1/4 inch thick
salt and freshly ground pepper
2 (5-ounce) bags baby spinach
2 tablespoons plain dry breadcrumbs
4 (6-ounce) boneless skinless chicken breasts
1/3 cup all-purpose flour, for dusting
½ cup pitted and sliced Spanish olives
2 tablespoons capers, drained
1 cup chicken stock
3 tablespoons unsalted butter, diced
2 tablespoons chopped flat-leaf parsley

Preheat oven to 375 degrees. Line a baking sheet with parchment. Drizzle olive oil on parchment, arranging lemon slices in a single layer. Drizzle lemons lightly with oil and season with salt and pepper. Roast for 20 minutes. The lemons will begin to brown. While lemons are baking, heat a large, deep skillet. Add spinach and cook over high, tossing until wilted, about 2 minutes. Transfer spinach to a strainer and press out liquid. Heat 2 tablespoons oil. Add breadcrumbs, cooking over moderate heat until toasted, about 1 minute. Add spinach, season with salt and pepper, and cook for 1 minute. In another deep skillet, heat remaining 1/4 cup oil. Season chicken with salt and pepper and dust with flour, shaking off excess. Cook chicken over high heat, turning once until golden, about 5 minutes. Add olives, capers and stock, bringing to a boil. Cook over high heat until stock is reduced by about two-thirds, about 5 minutes. Add lemons, butter, and parsley, and season with salt and pepper, simmering about 1 minute. Transfer chicken to plates and spoon sauce over.

Oven-Fried Chicken

Serves 6-8

I made this American favorite from *Celebrate Chicago*, in 2000 for visiting Swedish relatives.

    8 skinless half chicken breasts
    3 cups low-fat milk
    6 egg whites
    3 tablespoons parsley
    1 teaspoon tarragon
    3 cloves garlic, minced
    6 teaspoons Worcestershire sauce
    ¾ teaspoon pepper
    1 cup plain yogurt
    ¾ cup cornflakes, crushed
    6 tablespoons cornmeal

Rinse chicken and soak in milk. Mix egg whites, parsley, tarragon, garlic, Worcestershire sauce, pepper, and yogurt. Remove chicken from milk. Brush with yogurt mixture. Roll in corn flakes. Dust with cornmeal. Place in a baking dish sprayed with nonstick cooking spray. Bake at 375 degrees for 45–55 minutes, until chicken is tender.

Ginger and Orange Curried Fried Chicken

Serves 6

This recipe from *Casual Occasions* is complemented by saffron. (Pasta, Rice and Vegetables)

    12 half chicken breasts
    2 cups buttermilk
    2 tablespoons peeled fresh grated ginger
    3 tablespoons orange zest
    salt and pepper
    1 1/2 cups all-purpose flour
    4–5 teaspoons curry powder
    1/4 teaspoon ground ginger
    pinch cayenne pepper (optional)
    peanut oil for frying

In a shallow glass dish, combine buttermilk, grated ginger, orange zest, and salt and pepper. Mix well. Cover and marinate chicken for 1–2 hours in the refrigerator.

In a large paper bag, combine flour, curry powder, ground ginger, salt and pepper to taste, and cayenne pepper, if using. Remove chicken from marinade and, a few pieces at a time, shake in the bag of coating evenly in the seasoned flour.

Place a large frying pan over medium heat and pour oil to a depth of 3 inches, or until a small cube of bread turns golden within moments. When the oil is ready, add chicken and fry, turning once, until golden brown, 2–4 minutes on each side.

Using a slotted spatula, transfer to paper towels to drain briefly. Arrange on a warmed platter or on individual plates, and serve immediately.

Pan Roasted Chicken Breast

Serves 4

Bob, Erik, Karl, a music friend of Erik's and I spent Thanksgiving in New Orleans in 1990. Kris was in college at Oregon State and spent the holiday with friend Jeremy in Oregon City. One of the new cutting edge restaurants was Susan Spicer's Bayona. This recipe is from her 2007 cookbook *Crescent City Cooking*,

    4 chicken breasts, skinned
    salt and pepper
    2 tablespoons olive oil
    1 cup chicken broth
    6 tablespoons apple cider vinegar
    2 tablespoons unsalted butter, softened
    2 teaspoons Dijon mustard
    2 teaspoons coarsely chopped tarragon leaves
    2 teaspoons fresh chives, snipped

Preheat oven to 325 degrees. Season the chicken breasts with salt and pepper. Heat oil in a large skillet over medium-high heat. When almost smoking, add chicken breasts. Lower heat to medium and cook breasts 6–7 minutes. Turn the golden brown pieces and continue cooking for 5 minutes more. Rotate skillet if the heat is uneven and reduce heat if the chicken seems to be browning too quickly. When the chicken is cooked, remove to a platter and keep warm in the oven (don't cover). Pour excess grease from the pan and deglaze with the stock and vinegar, whisking to scrape up the browned bits on the pan's bottom. Let the liquid bubble briskly in the pan, whisking until it is reduced to about 1/2 cup. Then whisk in the butter, mustard, and tarragon.

The sauce should have a slightly creamy consistency. If it's too acidic, whisk in a little more butter or stock. Remove it from the heat and spoon over the chicken breasts. Sprinkle with chives.

Tandoori Chicken

Serves 6

This recipe for chicken on skewers is an excellent choice for a summertime barbeque. The marinade may also be used for shrimp. It is from The *Casual Occasions* cookbook by Chuck Williams. Joyce Goldstein was the owner/chef of Square One.

6 chicken breasts, cut into 1 1/2-inch cubes
2 cloves garlic, minced
1 (2-inch) piece of fresh ginger, cut up
3 tablespoons fresh lemon or lime juice
1/4 teaspoon turmeric
1 tablespoon cumin
2 fresh jalapenos, seeded and minced
1 cup nonfat plain yogurt
1 tablespoon paprika, for garnish
1/2 teaspoon salt
Lemon or lime wedges for garnish

In a food processor combine garlic, ginger, lemon or lime juice, turmeric, cumin, salt, jalapenos, and yogurt. Process until well blended. Transfer to a glass bowl. Add chicken and toss coating evenly. Cover. Marinate in refrigerator for 4–5 hours.

Place 12 bamboo skewers in water to cover, soaking 15–30 minutes. Prepare a fire in a grill. Drain the skewers. Remove chicken from the marinade. Put chicken on skewers and place on an oiled grill rack. Grill for 2 minutes. Turn and grill until the chicken is opaque at the center, about 2 minutes longer. Sprinkle with paprika and serve immediately with lemon or lime wedges.

Asian Diced Chicken with Lettuce Cups

Serves 6

I ordered a similar entrée at our favorite Chinese restaurant on Valencia Avenue in Fullerton.

1 pound chicken breasts, finely diced
1/2 cup soy sauce
2 teaspoons cornstarch
7 tablespoons sesame oil, divided
pepper to taste
1/2 cup olive oil
4 cloves garlic, minced, divided
1/2 cup diced water chestnuts
1/2 cup diced onion
1/2 cup diced green onions
1/4 cup chopped cilantro
1/2 teaspoon oyster sauce
1 teaspoon sugar
6 tablespoons toasted pine nuts
hoisin sauce
6 lettuce or radicchio cups

Combine soy sauce, cornstarch, 6 tablespoons sesame oil, and pepper in a medium bowl. Add diced chicken. Let stand 30 minutes at room temperature. Remove chicken from marinade.

Heat skillet over high heat. Add olive oil. Add half of the garlic to chicken mixture. Stir-fry 3 minutes. Remove chicken onto a plate. Remove all but 2 tablespoons oil from skillet. Add remaining garlic and stir-fry until golden. Add water chestnuts, onion, green onions, and cilantro. Stir-fry 1 minute. Remove all but 2 tablespoons oil from skillet. Add remaining garlic and stir-fry until golden. Add water chestnuts, onion, green onions, and cilantro.and stir-fry 1 minute. Add remaining soy sauce, oyster sauce, sugar, and remaining 2 teaspoons sesame oil. Stir-fry 2 minutes. Add pine nuts and chicken mixture. Heat 1 minute. To serve, spread Hoisin sauce in lettuce or radicchio cups. Top with chicken mixture. Roll up. Place on 6 plates.

Grilled Chicken Chardonnay

Serves 8

Barbequed chicken is a popular entrée in our family, especially when one of our sons visits. This marinade, from *Nordstrom's Friends and Family Cookbook* is both interesting and unusual.

   8 boneless, skinless chicken breast halves
   1 cup extra virgin olive oil
   3/4 cup chardonnay
   1/4 cup fresh lemon juice
   3 cloves garlic, finely chopped
   2 tablespoons coarsely chopped rosemary
   1 tablespoon dried oregano
   2 teaspoons kosher salt
   1 teaspoon freshly ground black pepper
   vegetable oil, for brushing

Place chicken in a 1-gallon lock-top plastic bag or a baking dish. In a bowl, combine olive oil, wine, lemon juice, garlic, rosemary, oregano, salt and pepper, and whisk until thoroughly blended. Pour marinade over the chicken, coating all sides well. Squeeze all the air out of the bag and seal, or cover the dish. Refrigerate and marinate the chicken a minimum of 4 hours or up to 24 hours. Turn the bag or the chicken breasts once to distribute the flavors evenly. Remove from the refrigerator 30 minutes prior to grilling.

Prepare a medium fire in charcoal grill, or preheat gas grill medium.

Remove the chicken from the marinade and drain excess marinade. Brush the grill grate with vegetable oil. Place the chicken directly over the fire. Cover the grill and cook on one side for about 2 minutes. Turn the chicken about 90 degrees to create attractive cross-hatching and cook for 2 minutes longer. Flip the chicken breasts over and continue grilling, covered, until tender and the juices run clear when the meat is pierced with a knife, about 4 minutes longer. Serve immediately.

Chicken Divan

Serves 4

I made this recipe often when the boys were young. I first had it in 1965 with my mother in Palo Alto.

   2 cups chicken slices, cooked
   1 package frozen broccoli, partially cooked
   4 tablespoons butter
   4 tablespoons flour
   1 cup whole milk
   1 can chicken consommé, undiluted
   salt, pepper, and paprika to taste
   1/4 cup Parmesan cheese

Mix butter, flour, milk, chicken consommé, salt, pepper, and paprika together. Place cooked chicken and broccoli spears in a greased baking dish. Cover with the cream sauce. Bake in 350 degree oven for about 30 minutes or until brown and bubbly. Top with cheese.

Roast Turkey with Smoked Sausage Stuffing

Serves 8–10

This recipe is placed here since there isn't a stuffing category.

12 slices homemade-type white bread
3/4 pound Kielbasa sausage, chopped
1 cube (1/2 cup) unsalted butter
1 1/2 cups onion, chopped
1 1/2 cups celery, chopped
2 large garlic cloves, chopped
2 teaspoons crumbled dried rosemary
1 cup scallions with tops, thinly sliced
1/3 cup minced parsley
1 teaspoon salt
1/8 teaspoon cayenne, or to taste
1/2 teaspoon black pepper

Bake bread slices in one layer on baking sheets in preheated 300- degree oven for 10–20 minutes. Cool. Enclose in plastic bag and crush until coarse. Transfer to large bowl. In a large skillet, cook sausage, stirring until some of fat has rendered and sausage is golden. Transfer sausage with a slotted spoon to bowl of crusts. Add butter to fat remaining in skillet. Melt and add onion and celery. Cook over moderately low heat, stirring until vegetables are softened. Add garlic and rosemary, cooking for 1 minute. Transfer mixture with butter to crumbs. Add scallion, parsley, salt, cayenne, and pepper, combining the stuffing well. Let cool completely *(Stuffing may be made up to 1 day in advance if kept covered and chilled.)* Do not stuff turkey in advance.

Chicken, Snow Peas, and Cashews

Serves 4–6

This quick to prepare entrée is perfect for a weekday dinner. I first saw it in *Sunsational,* a Florida Junior League cookbook that Karl gave to me for Christmas in 1983.

2 pounds boneless chicken breasts, diced
2 tablespoons canola oil, divided
10 ounces frozen pea pods
1 cup fresh mushrooms, sliced
1 cup cashews, chopped
2 tablespoons soy sauce

In a large skillet, quickly cook chicken pieces in 1 tablespoon of oil. Remove chicken and set aside. Add 1 more tablespoon of oil. Cook peas and mushrooms. Add chicken and cashews to vegetables. Add soy sauce and cook 2 minutes, until well mixed and heated thoroughly.

Hot Crunchy Chicken

Serves 4–6

Charleston Receipts Repeats is a cookbook I purchased when Karl spent the year in Charleston after finishing his Masters at the University of Florida in Gainesville. He spent the year writing and working at the restaurant Arizona before beginning his PhD studies at UCLA.

    2 cups diced cooked chicken
    1 can cream of chicken soup, undiluted
    1 cup almonds, slivered
    2 ounces fresh mushrooms, diced
    1/2 cup crushed Ritz crackers
    1/2 cup crushed potato chips

Preheat oven to 375 degrees. Combine all ingredients except potato chips. Spoon into a greased 1 1/2-quart baking dish. Bake for 15 minutes. Sprinkle top with potato chips. Bake an additional 15 minutes before serving.

Meat

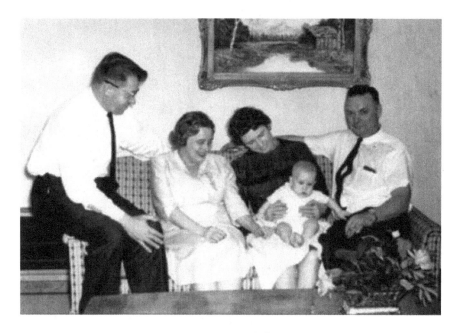

Sacramento, California

*Home (means) the house, but also everything in
it and around it, as well as the people.*

—Witold Rybezynski

Our Family Recipe – London Broil I

Serves 4

I have prepared this steak since the 1970's and it is our favorite.

    1 1/2 pounds flank steak
    1/2 cup sherry
    1/2 cup soy sauce
    2 cloves garlic, chopped
    1/2 cup fresh ginger or 1 teaspoon ground ginger

Slash diagonal lines in meat on both sides. Combine the marinade ingredients and marinate steak a minimum of 4 hours, turning meat periodically or a maximum time of overnight. When ready to cook, place meat on a broiler pan and broil for 4 minutes each side. Meat should be rare on inside.

Spice Rubbed Grilled Flank Steak II

Serves 4

This recipe, from a 2004 *Bon Appetit*, is excellent with Mixed Cherry Tomatoes with Tamarind Dressing (see Salads).

1 1/2 pounds flank steak
2 large garlic cloves
1 1/2 teaspoons peeled and grated ginger
1 teaspoon cinnamon
1 teaspoon kosher salt
1 teaspoon coriander
1/2 teaspoon pepper
1/2 teaspoon cumin

Mash garlic and ginger to a paste with salt and spices in a mortar and pestle. Pat steak dry. Rub paste all over steak and marinate, covered. Chill overnight. Prepare grill for cooking. Bring steak to room temperature (no longer than 1 hour). When fire is hot, grill steak on lightly oiled grill rack 5–8 minutes on each side for medium rare. Transfer steak to a cutting board and let stand 10 minutes. Holding knife at a 45-degree angle, cut steak across the grain into thin slices.

Grilled Mustard-Coated Flank Steak III

Serves 8

Our family loves flank steak. This is a different marinade.

2 flank steaks, 1 1/2–2 pounds each
1 cup mixed mustards, Dijon and grained
1/4 cup olive oil
2 teaspoons dried thyme
2 teaspoons dried oregano
2 teaspoons dried rosemary
2 teaspoons dried basil
4 garlic cloves, minced

Combine mustards with olive oil, herbs, and garlic. Coat steaks with mixture, refrigerating covered overnight. Remove from refrigerator 1 hour before cooking. Prepare a barbecue, and grill flank steaks over a hot fire for 5 minutes on each side, until medium rare. Remove to a cutting board. Cover with aluminum foil and let rest 10 minutes. Slice in thin diagonal slices across the grain, and serve immediately.

Tamale Pie

Serves 6

I remember my mother making this in Fresno (1945-1951).

  1 1/2 cups corn meal
  1 cup Mazola salad oil
  1 #2 can tomatoes
  1 16 ounce can cream style corn
  1 medium green pepper, chopped
  1 clove garlic, chopped
  1 teaspoon chili powder
  1 onion, chopped
  1 teaspoon salt
  1/4 pound ground pork
  3/4 pound ground beef
  1 small can black olives, sliced

Put 1/2 cup oil in a kettle; put the other 1/2 cup oil in a frying pan adding garlic, onion, pepper, and meat. Cook for 20 minutes and drain fat. In the kettle, put the corn, tomatoes, and cornmeal. Stir and cook for 15 minutes. Combine the two and season. Add olives and put in a loaf pan. Bake for 45 minutes at 350 degrees.

Washington Dog Breath Chili

Serves 8-10

I purchased the *Tyee Cookbook* at the Rose Bowl. Bob and I watched the Huskies play with friends Denny and Judy Sullivan.

3 pounds ground beef
1 pound sirloin, cubed
1 1/2 onions, chopped
1 green pepper, chopped
2 stalks celery, chopped
3 cloves garlic, minced
3 green or yellow chili peppers
1 (16-ounce) can stewed tomatoes
1 (6-ounce) can tomato paste
salt and pepper to taste
1 (15-ounce) can tomato sauce
1 (7-ounce) can chili salsa
1/2 can beer
3 ounces chili powder
pepper and oregano

Cook the onion, green pepper, and celery in enough oil to cover the bottom of a Dutch oven. Add meat and brown, cooking 15 minutes.

Remove excess grease. Add remaining ingredients, sprinkling pepper and oregano to cover the top of the chili. Simmer 2 1/2 hours, stirring often.

Butterflied Leg of Lamb with Juniper Berries and Rosemary

Serves 8

We enjoyed this in Fullerton by our pool on several Easter Sundays. Leg of lamb was my father's favorite meat. Bob thought he didn't like lamb. One time early in our marriage I whispered to my mother to not tell Bob the entrée was lamb. She didn't, and he loved it.

1 (6-8 pound) leg of lamb, butterflied
olive oil
1 teaspoon coarse salt
1/3 cup juniper berries
2 teaspoons black peppercorns
2 tablespoons fresh shredded rosemary

(Note: Have the butcher pound the thicker portions of the lamb, so that all of the meat will be the same thickness and will cook evenly.) Rub the lamb with olive oil to coat and sprinkle with salt. Crush the juniper berries and peppercorns with a mortar and pestle or in a spice grinder. Combine with the rosemary and press into the lamb, turning to coat thoroughly. Refrigerate for 4–6 hours.

Cook on a very hot barbecue grill, turning once or twice for 30–40 minutes, until the meat registers 130–135 on a thermometer. The meat should be crusty on the outside and pink inside. Let sit for 15 minutes before carving. Cut against the grain into thin diagonal slices and serve with its own juices.

Stuffed Peppers

Serves 6

This casual dinner entrée has been a staple in our family since our second year of marriage. It is from *The Spice Islands Cookbook* published in 1961. I still make it now in 2014. Bob loves it!

3 large green peppers
3 tablespoons minced onions
3 tablespoons water
1 pound ground lean ground beef
1/2 cup quick-cooking rice
1/2 teaspoon salt
1 teaspoon oregano
1 teaspoon basil
2 (8-ounce) cans tomato sauce
1/2 cup hot water
1/2 cup dry white wine
1-1 1/2 cups shredded sharp cheddar cheese

Split green peppers in half, lengthwise. Remove seeds and stems. Drop into a large pot of boiling salted water. Turn off heat and let stand for 5 minutes. Drain. Arrange peppers in a baking dish. Mix onions with ground beef, rice, salt, oregano, basil, and 1 can tomato sauce. Fill peppers with meat mixture. Combine 1 can tomato sauce with hot water and wine. Pour over stuffed peppers. Cover with foil and bake in a 350 degree oven for 40 minutes. Uncover. Sprinkle with shredded cheese and continue baking for 20 minutes longer. Serve hot.

Spaghetti Pies

Each pie serves 6

From *Soupcon*, a Chicago Junior League cookbook I purchased in 1982 in Evanston when Karl was a freshman at Northwestern.

12 ounces spaghetti
1/2 cup butter
1 cup grated Parmesan cheese
3 eggs, well beaten
2 1/2 pounds ground beef
1 cup finely chopped onion
2 (15-ounce) cans tomato sauce
2 (6-ounce) cans tomato paste
2 teaspoons sugar
1/3 cup water
1 tablespoon oregano
garlic salt to taste
basil to taste
2 cups sour cream
8 ounces shredded mozzarella cheese

Cook spaghetti al dente. Drain. Stir in butter, Parmesan cheese, and eggs. Chop well with knife and fork. Form into a "crust" in 2 buttered 10-inch pie tins. Let cool.

Cook ground beef and onion; drain off fat. Stir in tomato sauce and paste, sugar, water, and other seasonings. Heat through. Spread sour cream on bottom of spaghetti "crusts." Fill pies with meat sauce. Cover with mozzarella. Bake at 350 degrees for 30 minutes.

Chilies En Nogada

Serves 6

I enjoyed this at the Red Cabbage Cafe in Puerta Vallarta, Mexico on a family trip with Erik, Laura, Marin, Anders, Kris, Toni, Alexander, and Bob. We loved the picturesque ocean setting.

Chilies

12 poblano chilies
1 tablespoon vegetable oil
1/2 onion, sliced
1 teaspoon oregano
1 large bay leaf, crushed
1 sprig fresh basil
1/2 cup vinegar
1 teaspoon salt

Chili filling

10 ounces ground pork
10 ounces ground beef
2 cups water
2 sticks cinnamon
2 bay leaves, crumbled
1 teaspoon oregano
1 large onion, diced finely
4 ounces almonds, finely chopped
3 carrots, shredded
2 zucchini, shredded
2 medium tomatoes, diced
1/4 red cabbage, shredded
2 cups potatoes, shredded
1/2 cup candied pineapple

1 cup bottled marinated vegetables
4 ounces almonds, finely chopped
4 ounces raisins
2 ounces pine nuts
1/2 cup sugar
1 teaspoon salt
1 tablespoon chicken consommé powder

Sauce

1 cup heavy cream
1 cup milk
2/3 cup sugar
12 ounces walnuts, shelled and diced
pomegranate seeds, for garnish

For Chilies

Roast and peel chilies. Rinse and pat dry. Heat vegetable oil and add onion along with oregano, bay leaf and basil, all tied together in cheesecloth. Add chilies. Sauté briefly. Add 1/2 cup vinegar and salt. Cover, lower flame, and simmer for 20 minutes. Remove from heat and let cool. Remove chilies to a plate, discarding vegetables and herbs. Refrigerate.

Cook meat in water, seasoned with cinnamon sticks. Add oregano and bay leaves tied in cheesecloth. Add onion,almonds,. Shred carrots and zucchini. Dice tomatoes. Finely chop marinated vegetables, Add to the meat along with almonds, raisins, pine nuts, 1/2 cup sugar, consommé powder, and salt. Lower flame. Cover and simmer 20 minutes. Remove cinnamon sticks and bag of herbs. Cool and refrigerate.

In a blender, purée the cream, milk, 2/3 cup sugar, and walnuts. If too thick, thin with half and half to a creamy consistency. Spoon filling into each chili. Place 2 chilies on each plate. Pour the walnut sauce over chilies. Sprinkle with pomegranate seeds.

Souvlakia Greek Shish Kebab I

Serves 6

Our favorite marinade is from the 1960 James Beard *Treasury of Outdoor Cooking.*

   3 1/2 pounds leg of lamb, cut into cubes
   1 large onion, finely chopped
   juice of 2 lemons
   1/2 cup olive oil
   2 bay leaves, crushed
   1 1/2 teaspoons salt
   12 grinds of peppermill
   1/2 cup parsley, chopped
   1 1/2 teaspoons oregano
   2 cloves garlic, chopped

Marinate 4 hours to overnight. Remove pieces of lamb from marinade and skewer with wedges of firm tomato and small squares of onion for at least 30 minutes before broiling. Brush with marinade during cooking, being sure to get a pleasant color on all sides.

Armenian Lamb Shish Kebab II

Serves 6–8

Our family loved Hagopian's shish kebab in Visalia. When we visited my parents, Bob and I always purchased several pounds of the meat to take home. This recipe is said to be similar.

- 2 pounds boneless leg of lamb, cut into 1 1/2-inch pieces
- 3 small onions, peeled and quartered
- 2 tomatoes, diced
- 3 tablespoon lemon juice
- 5–6 thin slices of lemon
- 1/2 cup extra virgin olive oil
- 1/3 cup dry red wine or sherry
- 4 large garlic cloves, minced
- 2 teaspoons dried bay leaves, cut into fine pieces
- 1/2 teaspoon freshly ground pepper
- 1 1/2 teaspoons sea salt

In a large stainless steel or ceramic bowl, place the lamb, onions, tomatoes, and lemon slices. Combine remaining ingredients and pour over the lamb. Cover and marinate in refrigerator for about 6 hours, turning to mix occasionally.

Drain marinade and reserve in a saucepan. Bring to a boil for 10 minutes; allow to cool.

Thread meat and vegetables onto skewers and broil in oven or grill 3–4 inches above white-hot coals, turning frequently until evenly browned. Baste with marinade. Broil or grill for 15–20 minutes, or until done as desired.

Ground Beef with Noodles

Serves 8–10

This may be prepared in advance, refrigerated, and cooked before serving.

2 pounds lean ground beef
12 ounces tomato sauce
10 ounces tomatoes and green chilies
1 teaspoon oregano
salt and pepper to taste
1 tablespoon sugar
16 ounces sour cream
8 ounces cheddar cheese, grated, divided
8 ounces cream cheese, softened
16-ounce package large noodles

Brown meat. Add sauce, tomatoes, green chilies, oregano, salt, pepper, and sugar. Simmer for 20 minutes. Mix sour cream, 2/3 of cheddar cheese, and cream cheese. Cook noodles as directed. In a baking dish, layer the beef, meat sauce, noodles, and cheese mixture. Repeat, ending with meat sauce. Garnish with remaining cheese. Cover and bake at 350 degrees for 30 minutes.

Meat Loaf in Sour Cream Pastry

Serves 6–8

I first made this unusual meatloaf for an Emanuel Lutheran Church event in the late 1970's. This Finnish recipe is from *Scandinavian Cooking*.

Sour cream pastry dough

2 1/4 cups flour
1 teaspoon salt
12 tablespoons chilled butter
1 egg
1/2 cup sour cream

Filling

4 tablespoons butter
1/4 pound mushrooms, chopped
3 pounds ground meat; beef and veal, or a combination
1 medium onion, chopped
1/4 cup parsley, chopped
1 cup cheddar cheese, grated
1/2 cup milk
1 egg
2 tablespoons milk, for dough

Sift flour and salt together in a large bowl. With two knives, cut in the butter until mixture resembles coarse meal. In a separate bowl mix the egg and sour cream. Add this to the flour mixture until the dough forms a soft, pliable ball. Wrap the dough in wax paper and refrigerate for 1 hour. Next, divide dough and roll out each half to a rectangle 6 x 14 inches. Save tiny scraps of dough. Butter the bottom of a flat cookie sheet. Put one sheet of the pastry on the sheet.

Melt butter in a 12-inch skillet. Add mushrooms and cook for 6–8 minutes, until lightly colored. Add meat, and continue to cook until the meat loses all trace of pink color. Combine the mushrooms, meat, onion, parsley, cheese, and milk in a large mixing bowl. Form the meat mixture into a ball and put it in the center of dough that has been placed on the cookie sheet. With your hands, very gently pat the meat into a loaf shape. Cover this with the second piece of pastry dough and seal the edges with a fork. Moisten the dough with a pastry brush dipped in the egg and milk. Prick holes in the top of the loaf to allow steam to escape. Roll out the scraps of dough and cut them into strips. Crisscross these over the top of the loaf to form a design. Again brush it with the egg and milk mixture. Bake at 375 degrees for 45 minutes, or until the pastry is golden brown.

Smoky Meat Loaf with Prune Ketchup II

Serves 8–10

From *Food & Wine* in 2007, this is by Chef Grant Achatz of Alinea.

Meatloaf

- 1 tablespoon celery seeds
- 1 tablespoon fennel seeds
- 1 tablespoon black peppercorns
- 1 star anise pod, broken
- 2 tablespoons vegetable oil
- 1 cup pumpernickel breadcrumbs
- 1 white onion, diced
- 1/4 cup minced fennel bulb
- 1 garlic clove, minced
- 1 small celery rib, minced
- 2 tablespoons smoked Spanish paprika
- 1 pound sliced bacon, chopped
- 3 pounds ground beef
- 3 large eggs, beaten
- 1/2 cup unsalted pistachios
- 1/4 cup maple syrup
- Kosher salt

Preheat oven to 350 degrees. Grind together celery and fennel seeds, peppercorns, and star anise. In a large skillet, heat oil. Add onion, minced fennel, celery, garlic, paprika and ground spices. Cook over low heat, stirring until vegetables soften, 8 minutes. Cool to room temperature. In a food processor, pulse bacon until finely ground. In a large bowl, mix bacon with ground beef. Mix in eggs and maple syrup, followed by vegetables, breadcrumbs, pistachios, and salt.

Pat the meat mixture into two 9 x 4-inch loaves and set them on opposite sides of a large-rimmed baking sheet. Bake for 1 hour or until thermometer inserted in the center of each loaf registers 160 degrees. Let rest for 10 minutes. Cut loaf into thick slices. Serve with Prune Ketchup. May be refrigerated up to 3 days.

Prune Ketchup

- 1 cup pitted prunes
- 1 cup water
- 1/4 cup unsulfured molasses
- 1/4 cup sherry vinegar
- 2 tablespoons sugar
- 1 star anise pod
- salt and freshly ground pepper

In a medium saucepan, bring ingredients to a boil. Simmer over moderate heat until prunes are soft, 20 minutes. Discard the star anise pod. Purée the ketchup in a food processor. Transfer to a bowl and season with salt and pepper. The ketchup may be refrigerated.

Market Meatloaf III

Serves 8

This dish was enjoyed by Art Alliance at lunch in Venice at Market Café.

Meatloaf

    3 tablespoons unsalted butter
    1/2 cup minced onion
    3/4 cup minced green onions
    1/2 cup minced carrot
    1/2 cup minced celery
    1/4 cup minced green pepper
    1/4 cup minced red pepper
    2 teaspoons minced garlic
    3 eggs beaten
    1 teaspoon salt
    1 teaspoon black pepper
    1/2 teaspoon white pepper
    1/4 teaspoon cayenne
    1/2 teaspoon cumin
    1/2 teaspoon nutmeg
    1/2 cup ketchup
    1/2 cup half and half
    1 1/2 pounds lean ground beef
    1/2 pound lean ground pork
    3/4 cup dry breadcrumbs

Gravy

    2 tablespoons butter, divided
    4 shallots, minced
    1 sprig thyme

1 bay leaf
dash of crushed peppercorn
1/2 cup chopped yellow bell peppers
1/4 cup chopped red bell peppers
1 cup dry white wine
1 cup beef stock
1 cup chicken stock
2 Roma tomatoes, diced
salt and pepper

For Meatloaf

Preheat oven to 375 degrees. Melt butter in a heavy skillet. Add onion, scallions, carrots, celery, bell peppers, and garlic. Cook until moisture has evaporated, 10 minutes. Set aside. Refrigerate covered about 1 hour. Combine eggs, salt, black pepper, white pepper, cayenne, cumin, and nutmeg, mixing well. Add ketchup and half and half, blending thoroughly. Add ground beef, ground pork, and breadcrumbs to egg mixture. Add chilled vegetables mixing thoroughly. Form mixture into a loaf pan and place pan inside of larger pan (11 x 13). Fill outside pan with boiling water about half way up sides. Place pan in the oven and bake for 35–40 minutes. Remove the loaf.

For Gravy

In a Dutch oven, melt 1 tablespoon butter, and sauté shallots, thyme, bay leaf, peppercorns, and bell peppers over medium heat for 3 minutes. Add wine and simmer over high heat until reduced by three quarters, to make glaze. Add beef and chicken stock and simmer uncovered until reduced by one fourth. Add tomatoes and bring to a slow simmer. Cook, covered, for 20 minutes. Stir in the remaining 1 tablespoon butter and season with salt and pepper to taste. Strain. Discard bay leaf and thyme before serving.

Spaghetti-Beef with Mixed Nuts

Serves 8–10

This recipe from *Sunset Casseroles* was loved by our sons. I took it to many Cub Scout potlucks and it was the first dish chosen.

1 (8-ounce) package spaghetti
2 large onions, finely chopped
2 tablespoons butter
2 pounds ground beef
2 teaspoons salt
1/2 teaspoon pepper
1 (10-1/2 ounce) can tomato soup
1 soup can water
1 (4-ounce) can sliced mushrooms
1/2 pound (8-ounce package) cheddar cheese, diced, divided
1 teaspoon sugar
2 tablespoons Worcestershire sauce
1 (7-ounce) can salted mixed nuts

Cook spaghetti in boiling salted water al dente. Drain. In a large pan, sauté onions in butter. Add ground beef. Season with salt and pepper. Stir in soup and water, mushrooms, 2/3 of cheese, sugar, and Worcestershire sauce. Mix in spaghetti. Cover and simmer 20 minutes. Put mixture into a greased casserole with coarsely ground nuts in center. Sprinkle with remaining cheese. Bake at 350 degrees for 30 minutes.

Filet Mignon with Gorgonzola Sauce

Serves 8

If you like steak, this well might become your favorite presentation. Thanks to Erik and Laura who found this recipe in the February 2007 issue of *Bon Appetit*.

    3 tablespoons olive oil, divided
    1/2 pound fresh shitake mushrooms, stemmed and sliced
    3 garlic cloves, minced
    1 1/2 cups whipping cream
    1 cup crumbled Gorgonzola cheese
    2 teaspoons chipotles in adobo
    8 (6-ounce) filet mignon steaks
    salt and pepper to taste

Heat 2 tablespoons oil in heavy large skillet over medium heat. Add mushrooms and sauté until soft, about 4 minutes. Add garlic and stir 1 minute. Add whipping cream and sauté until soft, about 4 minutes. Add garlic and stir 1 minute. Add whipping cream and bring to boil. Reduce heat to medium and simmer sauce until thickened, about 4 minutes. Stir in Gorgonzola cheese and chipotles. Season sauce with salt and pepper to taste. Make sauce 2 hours ahead and let stand at room temperature.

Sprinkle steaks with salt and freshly ground black pepper. Barbeque, putting small amount oil on steaks *or* heat remaining 1 tablespoon oil in another heavy large skillet Cook steaks until brown on both sides and cook to desired doneness, about 5 minutes per side for medium rare. Rewarm sauce. Transfer steaks to plates. Pour sauce over steaks and serve.

Stuffed Cabbage Rolls

Serves 8

I loved these when I first ordered them at Potluck on San Pablo Avenue in Berkeley in the 1960's. Opened by Chef Narsai David, the restaurant was Berkeley's first gourmet restaurant.

  1 head cabbage
  1 1/2 cup cooked rice
  1 pound country sausage
  1 pound lean ground beef
  1/2 onion, finely chopped
  1 egg
  1/2 teaspoon Worcestershire sauce
  1 teaspoon allspice
  1/2 teaspoon cumin
  1/2 teaspoon pepper
  1/2 cup beef broth
  2 (8-ounce) cans tomato sauce
  1 (8-ounce) carton sour cream
  salt and pepper to taste

Remove core from cabbage, separate leaves, removing center vein without splitting leaf. Steam cabbage or place leaves in boiling water until limp, about 1–3 minutes. Do not overcook cabbage

Combine rice, sausage, beef, onion, egg, Worcestershire sauce, allspice, cumin, pepper, beef broth, and 1 can tomato sauce. Mix well. Place 1/4 cup meat mixture on each cabbage leaf, rolling the filling inside the leaf like a burrito, sealing the mixture. Place rolls in a large casserole dish. Pour the remaining can tomato sauce over rolls. Cover pan and bake at 350 degrees for 1 1/2 hours. Baste rolls with sauce 2–3 times during baking. Serve with a dollop of sour cream.

Shaking Beef

Serves 4

Bob and I have had this unusual and delicious Vietnamese dish at Chef Charles Phan's Slanted Door on the Embarcadero in San Francisco. The restaurant won the James Beard award for outstanding restaurant in America in 2014

 1 pound filet mignon, cut into 1-inch pieces
 3 1/2 tablespoons sugar, divided
 1/3 cup plus 1 tablespoon canola oil, divided
 1 teaspoon kosher salt
 1 teaspoon ground pepper
 3 tablespoons soy sauce
 3 tablespoons fish sauce
 2 tablespoons white wine vinegar
 1 teaspoon rice wine
 6 scallions, cut into 1-inch pieces
 1 small red onion, thinly sliced
 3 garlic cloves, minced
 1 tablespoon unsalted butter
 watercress and lime for garnish

Toss meat with 1/2 tablespoon of sugar, 1 tablespoon of oil and 1 teaspoon each of salt and pepper. Let stand at room temperature for 1 hour. In another bowl, whisk remaining 3 tablespoons sugar with soy sauce, fish sauce, white wine vinegar, and rice wine.

Heat a large skillet until very hot. Add remaining 1/3 cup oil and heat until smoking. Add the meat, cooking over high heat undisturbed for 1 minute, until browned. Turn meat and cook for 1 minute longer. Tilt skillet and spoon off all but 1 tablespoon of oil. Scatter scallions, onion, and garlic over the meat and cook for 30 seconds. Stir soy mixture and add to pan, shaking to coat the meat; bring to a boil. Add butter, shaking until melted.

Line a platter with watercress. Pour the beef and vegetables on top. Serve with lime wedges.

Sauerbraten

Serves 6–8

Roasts were a staple at our late afternoon Sunday dinners in Fresno in the late 1940's. My mother's recipe for this roast was my favorite.

3-4 pound boneless rump roast
Salt to taste
2 tablespoons Crisco
2 yellow onions, sliced
1 bay leaf
1/4 cup water
1/2 cup red wine vinegar
1 tablespoon brown sugar
1/8 teaspoon cinnamon
1/4 teaspoon allspice
1/8 teaspoon ground cloves
1/2 cup seedless raisins
Additional water as needed
Mashed potatoes are a good accompaniment.

Sprinkle roast with salt. In a Dutch oven, brown in Crisco. Top roast with sliced onions and bay leaf. Combine water and vinegar and in this dissolve sugar and seasonings. Pour over meat. Cover and cook over low heat until almost tender, about 2 hours. Add more water as needed. Turn meat. Top with raisins. Cover and continue cooking until meat is tender, 30 minutes to 1 hour. Remove roast to platter to serve. Slice beef cross-grain and serve with mashed potatoes.

Soy Citrus-Marinated London Broil

Serves 6

This recipe is from *Gourmet Easy Dinners*, published in the summer of 2012. It is another flank steak variation.

London Broil

3/4 cup soy sauce
1/3 cup dry red wine
1/4 cup fresh lemon juice
1/3 cup fresh orange juice
3 tablespoons olive oil, divided
1 bunch scallions, cut into 3-inch lengths
5 garlic cloves, smashed and peeled
pinch of cayenne
1/2 teaspoon pepper
2 1/2–3 pounds top-round London broil diced into 1 1/2-inch pieces

Chipotle Mayonnaise

1 cup mayonnaise
2 teaspoons lemon juice
2 tablespoons chipotle chilies in adobe, chopped

In a 1-quart sealable plastic bag, combine soy sauce, red wine, juices, 2 tablespoons oil, scallions, garlic, cayenne, and 1/2 teaspoon pepper. Add steak and seal bag, turning to coat steak. Marinate, turning bag occasionally, at least 4 hours or overnight. Transfer steak to a plate, discarding marinade. Bring steak to room temperature, 30 minutes.

Prepare grill over medium-hot coals, moving to area of grill with no coals if flare-ups occur, until well browned, about 2 minutes per side. Grill, covered, turning the meat around until medium rare, 8–12 minutes longer. Transfer to a cutting board and let stand at least 15 minutes. Cut steak across the grain into thin slices. Transfer to a platter. Drizzle meat with juices accumulated on cutting board. Serve at room temperature with chilled mayonnaise that has been mixed with lemon juice and chipotle chilies in adobe.

Fish

San Jose, California

What a good shield a house is, emblazoned with the message that shared, daily life was lived within...

—Laurie Colwin

Sole en Papillote

Serves 6

I made this elegant recipe from the Time-Life cookbook *Great Dinners from Life* for a dinner party in Brea in 1969. I remember asking our butcher for a roll of "butchers" paper.

12 small Dover sole fillets
21 small mushroom caps, divided
3/4 cup butter, softened, divided
1/2 cup shallots, chopped
1 teaspoon salt
1/8 teaspoon white pepper
12 slices carrot
1 (5-ounce) split dry champagne
1 cup chicken broth, skimmed
1/2 cup flour
1/4 cup heavy cream
2 tablespoons lemon juice
2 tablespoons chopped parsley
1 egg white, slightly beaten
lemon wedges for garnish

Preheat oven to 350 degrees. Save the 12 best looking mushroom caps. Slice the other caps, arranging a few slices on the center of each fish fillet. Fold the ends of the fillets over the mushrooms. Spread one-quarter cup of butter in a baking pan. Sprinkle with shallots, salt, and pepper. Place fillets in pan, folded side down. Put the 12 remaining mushroom caps and the carrot in the pan. Pour in the champagne and chicken broth. Cover the pan with foil. Bring to a boil. Immediately place the pan in the oven and bake for 20 minutes.

While fish is baking, prepare *beurre manie* by mixing the remaining one-half cup butter with the flour. For the papillote, cut an oval about 20 inches long and 14 inches wide from one large piece of butchers' paper (or parchment). From another piece, cut another oval one inch bigger. Use the larger oval as the top. Generously butter the bottom sheet of paper to within one inch of the edge and put it on a cookie sheet. When the fish is baked, gently lift the fillets, mushroom caps, and carrot slices from the baking pan with a slotted spatula and set on a plate to drain. Cover with foil to keep warm.

Raise oven temperature to 400 degrees. Drain broth into a saucepan. Place over medium heat, adding the *beurre manie* a little at a time, stirring with a whisk until blended, smooth, and thick enough to coat the whisk lightly. Stir in cream and lemon juice.

Arrange drained fillets on the buttered bottom piece of paper. Garnish each with a mushroom cap, cut across the top to hold a carrot slice. Spoon about one cup of the sauce over the fillets. Sprinkle with parsley. Set the rest of the sauce aside to keep warm. Brush edges of both pieces of paper with egg white diluted with a little water. Put the second piece of paper on top and fold the bottom edge over the top edge, rolling them together and crimping them to get a tight seal. *(If paper tends to unwind, carefully stick a paper clip where needed, but don't forget to take it out before serving.)* Brush the edges and the top sheet with egg white. Bake for 10 minutes or until the paper gets crisp, puffs up and begins to brown. It can be kept waiting a reasonable amount of time, until the paper is torn open with a flourish to reveal the gastronomic feat, releasing the fragrance of the food inside. Serve with lemon wedges and pass the remaining sauce separately. Serve with boiled potatoes that have been dusted with parsley, and broccoli.

Grilled Salmon with Lime & Dill Butter

Serves 6

Timberline Lodge Cookbook is the source of this recipe. King salmon is preferred.

6 (6-ounce) salmon fillets
1 cup unsalted butter
2 teaspoons lime zest
2 tablespoons fresh lime juice
1/4 cup chopped fresh dill
salt and white pepper to taste

Mix the butter, lime zest, lime juice, dill, salt, and white pepper to taste. Chill in a bowl.

Grill salmon fillets 10 minutes per side. Serve with a heaping tablespoon of lime and dill butter on each serving.

Broiled Sea Bass with Orange-Pineapple Salsa

Serves 6

I have prepared this unique presentation of fish often.

Salsa

1 tomato, peeled
1/2 bunch cilantro
2 oranges, peeled and sectioned
1 small onion
8 serrano chilies
1/4 cup vegetable oil
1/2 teaspoon black pepper
1 cup pineapple chunks

Fish

6 ounces fresh fillet of sea bass
6 tablespoons unsalted butter, melted
6 cilantro sprigs

For Salsa

Dice all fruit and vegetables except the chilies to the same size. Chop the chilies, with their seeds very fine. Mix all the ingredients together. Chill until ready to serve.

For Fish

Broil (or grill) the fish fillets. Place one fillet on each dinner plate and brush with melted butter. Spoon a generous amount of salsa over the fish. Garnish each with a cilantro sprig. Boiled potatoes accompany well along with a vegetable.

Crab and Sherry in Shells

Serves 6

My mother and I had lunch in 1964 at a Palo Alto restaurant that supported the Stanford Children's Hospital. A recipe for this crab dish was in a box of recipes I purchased that day.

2 cans crab meat
2 hard-boiled eggs, chopped
1 teaspoon chopped parsley
2 teaspoons lemon juice
1 teaspoon grated onion
3 tablespoons sherry
1/2 teaspoon Worcestershire sauce
1/2 teaspoon prepared mustard
1/2 cup breadcrumbs, toasted and buttered

Mix all ingredients except crumbs together. Place in greased shells. Cover with crumbs and bake in 400-degree oven for 15 minutes

Chop Stick Tuna Casserole

Serves 4

My mother often made this entrée when I was growing up.

    1 cup can cream of mushroom soup
    1/4 cup water
    1 (13-ounce) can chow mein noodles, divided
    1 can tuna, drained
    1 cup celery, sliced
    1/2 cup salted and toasted cashews
    1/4 cup chopped onion
    pepper to taste

Combine soup and water; add 1 cup chow mein noodles, tuna, celery, cashews, and onion. Pepper to taste and toss lightly. Place in a greased 10 x 6-inch baking dish. Sprinkle remaining noodles on top. Bake at 375 degrees for about 15 minutes.

Kris's Cedar Plank Salmon

Serves 4–6

This may well be the very best preparation of salmon. Bob always requests Kris to serve it when we are in Portland or when Kris and Toni visit in Berkeley. He says the salmon must be wild and fresh.

    1-2 pound salmon fillet with skin, about 1 1/2-inches thick
    cedar grilling plank, about 14 x 6 inches
    2 tablespoons olive oil
    Kosher salt
    lemon juice
    dried rosemary to taste
    dill weed to taste
    pepper to taste
    honey
    butter
    2 lemons, sliced

Soak plank in water to cover for 2 hours, keeping it immersed. Prepare grill for direct-heat cooking over medium hot charcoal. Open vents on bottom and lid of charcoal grill. Drizzle the fillet with olive oil. Salt the fillet; squirt with lemon juice; Shake rosemary over fillet and then a bit of dill and pepper. Drizzle on a little honey. Add a few slivers of butter and lemon slices on top of fish.

Let marinated fish stand at room temperature for 15 minutes before cooking.

Put salmon on plank, skin side down. Grill, covered with lid until salmon is just cooked through and edges are browned, 13–15 minutes. Have salmon stand on plank 5 minutes before serving.

Battered Shrimp from Charleston

Serves 8

I ordered this entrée in Charleston in 2000 on an Art Guild trip.

Shrimp

 1 pound large shrimp, deveined
 8–10 cilantro leaves for garnish
 3 tablespoons scallions
 3 tablespoons sea salt

Place shrimp on paper towels and refrigerate. Fry cilantro leaves and scallions while shrimp is cooking.

Batter

 1 1/2 cups cornstarch
 1 1/2 cups all-purpose flour
 2 1/2 cups chilled soda water
 2 tablespoons white sesame seeds
 4 tablespoons black sesame seeds
 2 tablespoons sliced chives
 1 tablespoon minced parsley

Mix together cornstarch and flour. Add soda gradually until it forms a smooth thick batter. Add seeds and herbs. Keep cold and let rest.

Preheat oven to 350 degrees. Cut eggroll wrappers in half. Lay stacks on top of each other; cut in half diagonally. Blend together oils. Grease a cookie sheet. Place eggroll triangles on sheet brushing triangles with remaining oil mixture. Sprinkle with salt and 5-spice powder. Bake in preheated oven for 5–7 minutes until golden. Reserve.

Preheat frying oil to 350 degrees. Grab shrimp by tail, 3–4 at a time, and dip into batter. Place in hot oil. While shrimp are frying, drizzle the two sauces on plates. Remove shrimp from oil placing on absorbent paper. Season with sea salt. Stack shrimp, 5 each, and garnish with scallions and fried cilantro leaves. Put 2 flatbread triangles on top.

Mustard Sauce Hot Chili Garlic Sauce

- 1 cup honey
- 1 cup Dijon mustard
- 1 teaspoon sesame oil
- 4 tablespoons honey
- 2 teaspoons hot chili garlic sauce (sambal)
- 1 teaspoon rice wine vinegar

Mix together separately and reserve.

Chinese Flatbread

- 8 eggroll wrappers
- 1/4 cup olive oil
- 1 tablespoon sesame oil
- 1 tablespoon Chinese 5-spice powder
- salt and pepper to taste

Skillet Cajun Shrimp

Serves 4–5

The flavor of this spicy shrimp dish reminds me of a shrimp dish from Chicago's chef, Rick Bayliss. It is from the *Cha, Cha, Cha Cookbook* and was said to be the most popular entrée.

    1 pound shrimp, peeled and deveined
    1/2 cup Cajun Spice Mix (see below)
    1 1/2 cups dark beer
    2 cups heavy whipping cream
    1/2 teaspoon red pepper flakes

In a large, heavy saucepan, mix the Cajun spice mix and beer. Cook over medium heat, stirring constantly with a wire whisk to make a thick paste. Do not allow the mixture to burn. Gradually stir in the cream to make a smooth sauce. Cook over medium heat, stirring occasionally, 8–10 minutes or until sauce thickens slightly and turns a rich rust color. Add the shrimp and red pepper flakes. Reduce heat, and cook shrimp over low heat for 2–3 minutes or until the shrimp are pink and opaque. Taste and adjust seasoning. Serve on individual plates with a good French bread.

Cajun Spice Mix

Makes 1 1/2 Cups

1/2 cup sweet paprika
2 1/2 tablespoons cayenne pepper
1 1/2 tablespoon garlic powder
2 1/2 tablespoons onion powder
1 1/2 tablespoons white pepper
1 tablespoon dried thyme
1 tablespoon dried oregano
1 tablespoon salt

Combine all the ingredients and mix well. Store in an airtight container in a cool, dry place. Use as needed.

Sole Parmesan

Serves 2

This recipe is from Jake's in Portland. Bob and I first dined at this renowned northwest restaurant when Kris began OSU, and it became a regular for us for many years.

12–16 ounces sole, preferably Petrale
1/2 cup flour
1 egg, beaten
8 ounces shredded Parmesan cheese
1 cup dried breadcrumbs
3 tablespoons oil for frying
2 tablespoons butter
2 tablespoons lemon juice
6 lemon segments
2 teaspoons capers
1 teaspoon shallots, chopped
1 tablespoon parsley, chopped

Place flour, egg, and shredded Parmesan cheese, mixed with breadcrumbs in three separate baking dishes. Dip the fillets in flour first, shaking off excess, then into egg and finally in the cheese, taking great care to coat fish evenly and completely.

Heat the oil in a large non-stick pan or on a range top griddle over high heat. Place fish in pan and brown, about 1 minute. Turn fish, taking care not to disturb the crispy browned cheese. (If the coating flakes off in spots, remove the specks of cheese and scatter them back on top of the fish.) After turning, the fish will take only 1 more minute. Remove to plates.

Wipe oil from pan and return to stove. Add remaining ingredients, and cook over medium heat until the butter is slightly browned. Pour over fish.

Pecan-Crusted Fish with Citrus Meunière

Serves 4

This recipe is from Susan Spicer.

Pecan-Crusted Fish

4 fillets of snapper or trout
salt and pepper
1/2 cup pecan pieces
1/2 cup flour
1 teaspoon fresh thyme
1 teaspoon orange zest
1/2 teaspoon cayenne
1 egg
1/2 cup milk or buttermilk
3 tablespoons oil

Citrus Meunière (sauce)

3 tablespoons butter
1 tablespoon orange juice
1 tablespoon lemon juice
1 teaspoon chopped fresh parsley
salt and pepper to taste
tabasco sauce

For Pecan-Crusted Fish

Season fish with salt and pepper. Place pecans, flour, thyme, orange zest, and cayenne in a food processor, pulsing until well blended. Transfer mixture to a plate. In a shallow bowl, whisk egg and buttermilk. Dip fish into egg mixture, then pecan mixture. Coat fillets.

Heat oil in a large skillet over medium heat. When hot but not smoking, add the fish. Reduce heat to medium or medium-low and cook for 4–5 minutes on each side. Remove to a platter or plates. Keep warm while you make the sauce. Serve immediately.

For Citrus Meunière

Melt butter and let foam and turn golden brown. Pour in the juices and swirl the pan to mix. Add parsley; season with salt, pepper, and a few drops of hot sauce, and swirl. Spoon finished sauce over fish.

Petrale Sole in Herb Butter Sauce

Serves 4

This is another outstanding recipe for fish given by Kris to include in the cookbook.

- 1 1/2 pounds fresh Petrale sole fillets
- salt to taste
- 2 tablespoons olive oil
- 3 tablespoons minced shallots
- 1/4 dry white wine
- 2 tablespoons unsalted butter, cut into pieces
- fresh thyme leaves
- fresh chives, minced
- 2 teaspoons lemon juice
- lemon wedges as a garnish (Meyer lemons are preferable)

Pat sole fillets dry twice with paper towels. Lightly salt the fillets on both sides. Heat oil in a large, stick-free skillet on medium heat. Once the oil is hot, carefully add the fillets to the pan. Brown the fillets gently on both sides. Fish is cooked when it flakes easily and is no longer translucent. Sole fillets cook very quickly, no more than 2–3 minutes on each side. When done, remove the fillets from pan and place on a warm plate.

Add shallots to the skillet and sauté until soft. Deglaze the pan with white wine and scrape the browned bits at the bottom of the pan. Add butter and gently swirl to make a sauce. Add thyme leaves and chives, and squeeze 2 teaspoons lemon juice into the sauce. Spoon over the sole. Serve immediately.

✤ ✤ ✤

Curried Scallops

Serves 2

Bob and I both love scallops and I have made this recipe many times since living in Berkeley.

Curry Sauce

2 tablespoons butter
2 tablespoons finely diced onion
2 tablespoons flour
1 teaspoon curry powder
1/2 cup chicken broth1/2 cup cream
2 teaspoons orange zest
pinch of saffron

Scallops

12 jumbo sea scallops, cut into pieces
flour
2 tablespoons butter

For Curry Sauce

Melt butter over medium heat and sauté onions until they soften. Add flour and curry powder to form a roux. Add broth, cream, zest and saffron, and simmer until lightly thickened. Cook sauce for an additional 2–3 minutes, then reserve, keeping sauce warm.

For Scallops

Flour sea scallops lightly. Melt an additional 2 tablespoons butter in another pan and sauté scallops over medium heat for 3–4 minutes, turning once until golden brown. Place scallops on plates and pour curry sauce over them. Rice is a good accompaniment.

Rock Shrimp Dijon

This delicious and quick recipe makes a quick dinner.

  1/2 pound rock shrimp
  1 tablespoon butter
  2 green onions, sliced, about 3 tablespoons
  8–10 medium mushrooms, quartered
  2 teaspoons chopped shallots
  2 teaspoons chopped garlic
  2 tablespoons lemon juice
  1/2 cup cream
  2 tablespoons fresh basil, shredded
  2 tablespoons Dijon mustard

Melt butter over high heat. Add onions and mushrooms, and sauté for 1 minute. Add rock shrimp, shallots, and garlic. Sauté for an additional minute. Add remaining ingredients. Bring to a boil to reduce. Finish cooking for 1 more minute. If your sauce is not thick enough to coat a spoon, remove the shrimp and mushrooms to a serving plate and cook sauce for 1 final minute before pouring over the shrimp.

Grilled Garlic and Hot Pepper Shrimp

Serves 6

This shrimp entrée may be served with the Soy Citrus London Broil.

2 pounds shrimp, peeled and deveined
10 wooden skewers, soaked in warm water for 30 minutes
4 large garlic cloves, chopped
1/2 teaspoon red-pepper flakes
1/2 teaspoon fine sea salt
1/2 cup extra virgin oil

Pat shrimp dry, thread through top and tail leaving shrimp curled onto skewers, with no space between shrimp. Arrange skewers on a baking sheet.

Purée garlic with red-pepper flakes, salt, and oil. Transfer to a bowl; brush shrimp on both sides with spicy garlic oil. Broil shrimp 3–4 minutes turning once. Serve with chipotle mayonnaise.

Shrimp Cocktail

Serves 4-6

I love this shrimp cocktail. The salsa is from Frontera Grill.

1 pound small shrimp, peeled, deveined, and cooked
1/4 cup lime juice
1 cup Frontera Tomatillo Salsa
2 avocados, peeled and cubed
1/2 small red onion, chopped
1/4 cup chopped cilantro
2 tablespoons olive oil
1 jicama, diced
salt to taste
lime slices for garnish
corn tortilla chips for serving

Toss shrimp with the lime juice in a large bowl. Cover and refrigerate for 1 hour. Add salsa. Coarsely mash the pulp of 1 avocado and add to shrimp. In a small strainer, rinse onion under cold water. Shake off any excess liquid. Add to the shrimp, along with the cilantro, olive oil, and jicama. Taste and season with salt. Cover and refrigerate if not serving immediately, up to 4 hours.

Peel and dice the remaining avocado and gently stir into the shrimp mixture. Serve in yellow water goblets. (I purchased these at Neiman Marcus at the Stanford Shopping Center years ago. Laura and I had lunch and she decided on the items for her gift registry before she and Erik were married. Erik and Bob went hiking.)

Seared Scallops with Spinach, Bacon, and Tomatoes

Serves 4

You can't go wrong with food by Susan Spicer. This entrée is one I had at her restaurant on an Art Guild trip to New Orleans in 2010.

2 strips thick-sliced bacon, diced (preferably apple-smoked)
3/4 pound sea scallops
salt and pepper
2 tablespoons extra virgin olive oil
4 cups cleaned fresh spinach
1 garlic clove, minced
1 cup cherry tomatoes, halved
1 tablespoon minced shallots
2 tablespoons vinegar such as apple cider
1 tablespoon butter

Preheat oven to 200 degrees and place a large serving platter in the oven.

Cook bacon in a nonstick skillet over medium heat, stirring, until brown and crisp. Using tongs, remove bacon from skillet and drain. Pour the rendered fat into a small dish and set aside.

Rinse the scallops and pat dry. Season them lightly with salt and pepper on one side. Return the skillet to the stove, over high heat. When it is smoking, pour in the olive oil, then sear the scallops, seasoned side down, for 2–3 minutes, until crusty and light brown. Using a spatula, turn and sear them on the other side for a minute, then remove the scallops from the pan and cover them with foil to keep warm.

Return skillet to the stove, heat for 1 minute, then add the spinach and garlic and a pinch of salt. Stir with tongs or a spatula. When the spinach is wilted, remove it from the pan and pour off the excess liquid. Add the tomatoes and shallots to the pan and cook for 2 minutes. Add the vinegar and bring to a boil. Whisk in the butter and 1 tablespoon of the bacon fat and taste for seasoning.

To serve, place the spinach on the middle of the warmed platter. Using tongs, arrange the scallops and tomatoes around the spinach and drizzle with the warm sauce. Garnish with the bacon.

Pasta, Rice, and Vegetables

Brea, California

In a house which loves you, all things are possible.

—Marvin Bell

Noodles Romanoff

Serves 6–8

This recipe was given to me by Stella Anderson at whose home in Yuba City we were dinner guests when we lived in Sacramento. Her husband Roy was my father's oldest and closest friend from their childhood on adjoining Lodi farms

1 (8-ounce) package egg noodles
salt
1 cup large curd cottage cheese
1 small clove garlic, minced
1 teaspoon Worcester sauce
1 cup sour cream
1/4 cup grated onion
dash of Tabasco sauce
butter
1 (10 1/2-ounce) can tomato soup
salt and pepper to taste
½–1 cup grated cheddar cheese

Cook noodles until just tender in boiling salted water until tender. Combine drained noodles, cottage cheese, garlic, Worcester sauce, sour cream, tomato soup and grated onion. Add Tabasco sauce. Turn into a buttered casserole; sprinkle grated cheese over top. Bake at 350 degrees for 25 minutes. Add some chopped green pepper for color if you like.

Penne with Wilted Arugula, Radicchio, and Smoked Mozzarella

Serves 6

An excellent vegetarian entrée for a quick dinner.

1 pound penne
5 tablespoons extra virgin olive oil
1 teaspoon grated lemon zest
2 garlic cloves, minced
salt and pepper to taste
1 (6-ounce) head radicchio
6 cups (or 9 ounces) arugula, trimmed
1 cup fresh chopped basil
4 ounces smoked mozzarella cheese, cut into 1–2 inch pieces
2 tablespoons fresh lemon juice

Cook penne in pot of salted boiling water until al dente. While penne is boiling, whisk together oil, lemon zest, garlic, and salt and pepper to taste in a large bowl. Thinly slice radicchio, arugula, and basil. Add to dressing. Reserve 12 cups cooking water and drain penne into a colander. Add hot penne and reserved cooking water to greens and let stand 1 minute to wilt. Add smoked mozzarella and lemon juice, tossing well. Season with salt and pepper and serve warm.

Cheese Stuffed Baked Potatoes

Serves 8

My mother made these potatoes as far back as the 1940's.

6 medium potatoes, about 2 pounds
1 (8-ounce) package cream cheese
1/4 cup butter
1 tablespoon chopped green onion
1/2 teaspoon salt
dash of pepper
paprika

Bake potatoes at 400 degrees for 45 minutes. Remove from oven and knead gently. Slash the top, and scoop pulp from potato shells. Reserve shells. With a fork, mash pulp. Blend in cream cheese, butter, onion, salt, and pepper. Refill potato shells and sprinkle with paprika. Reheat at 400 degrees for 15–20 minutes.

Ortega Cheese Rice Casserole

Serves 8

My mother made this for Christmas Eve dinner and served it with sliced ham and homemade Christmas cookies for dessert.

  3 cups cooked rice
  2 (8-ounce) cans tomato sauce with mushrooms
  1 small can Ortega chili peppers
  2 small cartons sour cream
  2 cups grated Monterey Jack cheese
  1 cup Tillamook cheese
  black olives, sliced
  1 large bay leaf

Mix rice and tomato sauce. Put half into a casserole. Chop chilies, mixing with sour cream and bay leaf. Put half of chili/cream mixture on rice. Repeat layers. Place 2 cheeses on top. Bake at 350 degrees until cheese is melted and mixture hot. Garnish with olives. Serve.

Grant's Mac and Cheese

Serves 6

This recipe is the brainchild of revered Chicago chef, Grant Achatz.

1 pound elbow macaroni
1 tablespoon unsalted butter
6 thick slices of bacon (6 ounces), diced
1 medium onion, minced
2 bay leaves
1 tablespoon sweet paprika
1/2 teaspoon cayenne
1/2 cup flour
6 cups whole milk
5 cups extra-sharp cheddar cheese, shredded, divided

Preheat oven to 350 degrees. Butter a 9 x 13 x 2-inch dish. In a large saucepan, melt butter. Add bacon, and cook over moderate heat until crisp, about 7 minutes. With a slotted spoon, transfer bacon to a plate. Absorb excess fat with a paper towel. Add onion and bay leaves to the saucepan and cook over moderate heat, stirring occasionally, until onion is softened, about 5 minutes. Add paprika and cayenne and cook, stirring, until fragrant. Stir in the flour until blended. Gradually whisk in the milk until sauce is smooth. Bring to a boil over high heat, whisking constantly, and cook until thickened. Reduce heat to low and simmer gently for 30 minutes, whisking frequently. Discard bay leaves.

Bring a large pot of salted water to a boil. Add macaroni and boil until pliable but still undercooked, about 4 minutes. Drain macaroni and return it to the pot. Stir 4 cups of the cheddar cheese into the hot sauce. Add bacon and season with salt. Add sauce to the macaroni mixing well. Spread the macaroni and cheese in the baking dish, scatter the remaining cup of cheese, and cook until golden brown and bubbling. Let stand for 10 minutes before serving. May be made the day before serving and kept in refrigerator.

Paula's Mac and Cheese

Serves 6

A pasta favorite of our grandchildren, especially Anders. It is from *Food & Wine*, 2007.

3/4 pound elbow macaroni
3 cups shredded sharp cheddar cheese, divided
3 large eggs
1/2 cup sour cream
1 cup whole milk
4 tablespoons unsalted butter
1/2 teaspoon salt

Preheat oven to 350 degrees. Lightly butter an 8 x 12 inch baking dish. In boiling salted water, cook macaroni until al dente. Drain. Transfer to a bowl. Add 2 cups of cheese and toss until melted. In another bowl, whisk eggs with sour cream. Add milk, butter, and salt. Stir the mixture into macaroni and pour it into prepared dish. Sprinkle the remaining 1 cup of cheese on top. Bake for 35 minutes until bubbling and cheese has melted. Let the macaroni and cheese stand for 15 minutes before serving.

Cha, Cha, Cha Spanish Rice

Makes 4 cups

This unusual rice is from the *Cha Cha Cha* cookbook. I first made it for a surprise sixtieth birthday lunch for Gloria given by her daughters.

1/3 cup olive oil
1 tablespoon minced garlic
1/2 red bell pepper, minced to 1/4-inch pieces
1 green bell pepper, minced to 1/4-inch pieces
1 onion, diced
2 bay leaves
1/2 tablespoon white pepper
1 tablespoon salt
1/4 teaspoon turmeric
5 cups chicken stock
1 cup diced green Spanish olive
1 cup diced black olives
1 tomato, seeded and cut into 1/2-inch pieces
1 bunch cilantro, stemmed and diced
1 tablespoon capers
2 cups white long-grain rice

In a medium saucepan, heat olive oil and cook garlic, peppers, onion, and bay leaves until onion is translucent, about 2–3 minutes. Reduce heat, and add white pepper, salt, and turmeric. Stir in the chicken stock or broth, olives, tomato, cilantro, capers and then the rice. Bring to a boil; cover and lower heat to a simmer. Cook 20 minutes. The rice may be made one day earlier. When ready to serve, add more broth if necessary.

Individual Potato Soufflés

Serves 8

This recipe is from *Philadelphia Orchestra Cookbook*.

    6 baking potatoes
    4 tablespoons butter
    1 1/2 cups sour cream
    2/3 cup grated Parmesan cheese, divided
    salt and pepper to taste
    8 tablespoons sour cream, for topping, divided
    parmesan cheese, for topping
    paprika, for topping

Preheat oven to 400 degrees. Prick potatoes with a fork and bake for 1 hour. When cool, cut potatoes in half, scooping out insides. Put potatoes through a ricer or mash. Add butter, sour cream, 1/2 cup Parmesan cheese, and salt and pepper to taste. Divide mixture into individual greased baking dishes. Spread 1 tablespoon sour cream over each portion. Sprinkle with remaining cheese and paprika. May be made ahead to this point. Increase oven temperature to 450 degrees and bake uncovered for 30 minutes or until brown. Serve immediately.

Cilantro Rice

Serves 6

I had this rice in 1996 at the Santa Fe restaurant Café Pasqual on an Art Alliance art trip.

    1 1/2 cups long grain white rice
    2 cups water
    1 1/2 teaspoons kosher salt, divided
    1 cup loosely packed fresh cilantro
    1/2 cup chopped white onion
    1/4 cup chopped green onions
    1 1/2 tablespoons chopped jalapeno
    1 1/2 tablespoons fresh lime juice
    1 tablespoon olive oil

Bring rice, water, and 1 teaspoon salt to a boil in a 2-quart heavy saucepan. Reduce heat to low. Cover pan with tight-fitting lid. Cook 20 minutes. Remove from heat and let stand, covered for 5 minutes. Remove lid and fluff rice with a fork. While rice is cooking, purée cilantro, onion, green onion, jalapeno, lime juice, olive oil, and remaining 1/2 teaspoon salt in a blender. (If mixture is too dry, add 1–2 tablespoons water.) Add mixture to rice. Stir with a fork.

Saffron Rice

Serves 6

This fragrant golden yellow rice highlights fried chicken.

    2 cups basmati rice
    6 quarts water
    salt
    1/4 cup dry white wine
    1 teaspoon saffron threads
    6 tablespoons unsalted butter
    1 cinnamon stick
    8 whole cloves
    seeds from 8 cardamom pads
    pepper, freshly ground
    1/2 cup toasted almonds

Combine rice and water to cover by 1 inch. Let stand 2 hours. Drain. Preheat oven to 350 degrees. In a saucepan, bring 6 quarts of water to a boil with salt. Add drained rice, and boil for 10 minutes. Drain rice again, and rinse with warm water. Drain again. Place in a shallow 1 1/2 quart baking dish measuring about 9 x 11 x 2 inches.

In a small pan over low heat, warm the wine; remove from heat. Crush saffron threads gently, and add to the warm liquid. Let stand for 10 minutes. In a small frying pan, melt butter. Add saffron, cinnamon, cloves, cardamom, and pepper to taste, and toss with butter. Add mixture to rice, tossing well. Cover baking dish with aluminum foil. Bake until butter has been absorbed and rice is tender but still firm, about 25 minutes. Remove cinnamon stick and cloves and discard. The almonds may be added to the butter with the spices.

Tabbouleh

Serves 12

This Middle Eastern specialty is delicious! The recipe is from a Lawry's cookbook.

Lemon Garlic Dressing

3 tablespoons lemon juice
3 tablespoons water
1/2 teaspoon Lawry's Garlic Powder with Parsley
1/2 teaspoon sugar
1/2 teaspoon Lawry's Seasoned Salt
1 tablespoon finely minced parsley
1/2 teaspoon grated lemon peel
1/2 teaspoon dry mustard
1/4 teaspoon turmeric
dash Lawry's Seasoned Pepper
2/3 cup salad oil

For Lemon Garlic Dressing

Combine all ingredients except oil in a jar; shake well. Add oil and shake again for 30 seconds.

Rice

1/2 cup uncooked long grain brown rice
3/4 cup boiling water
2 large bunches parsley, chopped
1 bunch green onions, chopped
1 1/2 cups diced tomatoes
1/4 cup fresh chopped mint
juice of 1 lemon

For Rice

Cook rice in boiling water covered, for 5 minutes. Drain. Combine all ingredients including dressing. Refrigerate overnight.

Hot, Hot Potato Wedges

Serves 4

These spicy potatoes are excellent with roast chicken or lamb.

1/2 cup vegetable oil
4 large garlic cloves, pressed
3 tablespoons fresh lime juice
1 teaspoon chopped fresh thyme
2 teaspoons Tabasco sauce
salt to season
2 large russet potatoes, cut into wedges

Whisk first five ingredients in small bowl to blend. Season with salt. Arrange potatoes in a 13 x 9 x 2-inch glass baking dish. Season with more salt, if needed. Set aside 1/4 cup dressing. Pour remainder over potatoes and toss to coat. Let stand 30 minutes.

Preheat oven to 400 degrees. Roast potatoes until crisp and brown, turning occasionally, about 1 hour. Drizzle reserved 1/4 cup dressing over potatoes. Serve.

Mustard and Coriander Roasted Potatoes

Serves 6

These are especially good with flank steak.

    2 pounds russet potatoes, peeled and cut into 1 1/2 inch cubes
    1/4 cup Champagne vinegar
    2 tablespoons mustard seeds
    1 teaspoon Dijon mustard
    1 tablespoon coriander seeds, crushed
    1 teaspoon coarse kosher salt
    pepper
    6 tablespoons vegetable oil

Preheat oven to 425 degrees. Bring vinegar and mustard seeds to boil in a small saucepan. Reduce heat; simmer until almost dry, stirring occasionally, about 5 minutes. Transfer to a large bowl. Add mustard and coriander. Season with coarse salt and pepper. Place potatoes in large saucepan; add water to cover by 1 inch. Boil 3 minutes. Drain; return to pan. Cook over medium high heat until dry, shaking pan occasionally, 3 minutes.

Drizzle 6 tablespoons oil over large rimmed baking sheet. Place sheet in oven 10 minutes to heat. Add potatoes to mustard mixture; toss. Spread potatoes on hot baking sheet. (Be careful as oil may splatter.) Sprinkle with coarse salt and pepper. Roast 15 minutes; turn potatoes. Roast until browned and tender, about 15 minutes longer. Season with more coarse salt and pepper, as needed, and serve hot.

Mashed Potatoes with Leeks

Serves 6–8

I have served these mashed potatoes for Thanksgiving many times.

3 pounds russet potatoes
6 leeks (pale green parts only)
6 tablespoons unsalted butter, divided
1 teaspoon thyme
salt and pepper to taste
1 cup whole milk
1/2 cup whipping cream

In a large kettle, combine potatoes with cold water, covering by 2 inches. Bring water to boil and simmer, 35–45 minutes. Cook leeks in 4 tablespoons butter over moderate heat, stirring occasionally, until softened. Stir in thyme. Salt and pepper to taste. Drain potatoes and return to kettle. Dry over low heat, 1 minute. Cool until they can be handled. Peel warm potatoes and force through a ricer. In a small saucepan, beat milk and cream until mixture comes to a boil. Stir leeks and milk mixture into potatoes. Salt and pepper to taste. Spread potato mixture in a buttered 4-quart baking dish. Chill covered, 1 day. Preheat oven to 350 degrees. Dot potatoes with 2 tablespoons butter and bake, covered, about 15 minutes.

Red and Yellow Pepper Risotto with Fontina

Serves 4

Fontina is one of my favorite cheeses. The flecks of red and yellow pepper make this risotto attractive.

> 3 cups chicken stock or broth
> 2 tablespoons olive oil
> 1 large yellow onion, chopped
> 1 red bell pepper, seeded and diced
> 1 yellow bell pepper, seeded and diced
> 1 clove garlic, minced
> 1 1/2 cups Arborio rice
> 1/4 cup shredded Fontina cheese
> 1 tablespoon chopped fresh thyme
> salt and pepper to taste

Bring stock or broth to a simmer, keeping liquid hot. Warm olive oil in saucepan over medium-low heat. Add onion, sautéing until softened, 5 minutes. Add bell peppers and garlic, stirring until softened, 5 minutes. Add a small amount of stock or broth and rice, adjusting heat to maintain a simmer. Cook until liquid is absorbed, about 2 minutes. Continue adding liquid a little at a time, stirring constantly until rice is just tender and mixture is creamy, about 25 minutes longer. Add cheese and thyme and stir until the cheese melts. Season with salt and pepper. Spoon onto warmed plates.

Potatoes with Two Cheeses

Serves 6

These delicious potatoes are good with steak or chicken, or would make a meal by themselves.

    6 large russet potatoes
    1/2 cup whole milk
    2 teaspoons fresh minced rosemary
    6 tablespoons (3/4 stick) unsalted butter, divided
    8 ounces Roquefort cheese, crumbled
    coarse kosher salt
    pepper
    4 ounces Gruyère cheese, grated

Preheat oven to 350 degrees. Bake potatoes 30 minutes. Using fork, pierce potatoes in several places. Bake until tender, about 1 hour longer. Maintain oven temperature. Meanwhile, microwave milk and rosemary on high for about 45 seconds. Let steep 30 minutes.

Slicing lengthwise, cut top quarter off each potato. Scoop potato into large bowl, leaving about one-fourth of potato in skin. Scrape potato out of tops; discard tops. Coarsely mash potatoes. Add 4 tablespoons butter, mash. Mash in milk mixture, then Roquefort cheese (mixture will be slightly stiff). Season with kosher salt and pepper. Divide mashed potatoes among potato skins; transfer to rimmed baking sheet. Sprinkle Gruyère cheese over potatoes, pressing slightly to adhere. Dot with butter. May be made up to 4 hours ahead. Let stand at room temperature. Bake potatoes until hot and tops begin to brown, about 30 minutes.

Florida Rice

Serves 6

Karl gave me the cookbook *Sunsational* for one Christmas. It included this recipe.

1 cup Uncle Ben's Converted Rice
2 cups water
1 teaspoon salt
1 tablespoon butter
4 tablespoons orange juice concentrate
3 tablespoons golden raisins
2 tablespoons almonds, toasted and slivered

Bring 2 cups water to a boil. Stir in rice, salt, butter, orange juice concentrate, raisins, and almonds. Cover tightly and simmer 20 minutes. Remove from heat. Let stand, covered, until water is absorbed. Stir in more concentrate after rice is cooked, if needed.

Wild Rice

Serves 6

My mother prepared this rice. I first made it in 1966 in Brea.

1 1/2 cups S&W Wild Rice, washed
1/3 cup salad oil (Mazola)
1/2 cup chopped parsley
1/2 cup chopped green onions
1 cup celery, sliced
1 (10 1/2-ounce) can consommé
1 1/2 cups water
1 teaspoon salt
1/2 teaspoon thyme
1/2 cup sherry

Combine oil, parsley, onions, and celery, cooking until soft, but not browned, 10 minutes. Add 1 1/2 cups rice, consommé, 1 1/2 cups boiling water, salt, and thyme. Cook, covered over low heat, 45 minutes. Stir occasionally. When rice is tender and liquid absorbed, stir in sherry. Cook uncovered for 3 more minutes.

Savory Cheese Pie

Serves 6

This simple dinner entrée doesn't really fit into this category, but I wanted to include it. From Sunset's 1962 *Dinner Party Cookbook*, I first made it for friends Sidney and Jim Lowrey at our home on Carlson Drive in Brea about 1967. Perfect for Halloween.

Pastry for a double-crust 9-inch pie. Use *The Master Crust* recipe, leaving out the sugar.

   1/2 teaspoon black pepper
   1/4 teaspoon dry mustard
   1/4 teaspoon paprika
   1/2 pound sharp cheddar cheese, shredded
   2 eggs
   2/3 cup whole milk
   1/4 teaspoon salt
   1 1/2 tablespoons onion, finely chopped
   2 medium tomatoes, peeled and sliced
   1 beaten egg

Work pepper, mustard, and paprika into the pastry as you blend it. Divide pastry into 2 balls and roll out one; use to line a 9-inch pie plate. Distribute the shredded cheese in pastry lined pan. Beat eggs with milk, salt, and onion. Pour over cheese. Cover with a layer of tomato slices. Top with remaining rolled-out pastry, saving scraps of dough. Trim, crimp edges, and make slits in top. Make 2 or 3 leaves from scraps and place on center of pie. Brush top with beaten egg. Bake in a very hot oven, at 425 degrees for 10 minutes. Reduce heat to 325 degrees and bake 30 minutes longer or until browned. Serve hot.

Asparagus Risotto

Serves 4

I first had risotto in 1992 at a Santa Monica restaurant with Karl. It was delicious and wasn't on very many menus at the time. This recipe is from a Williams-Sonoma 2000 cookbook.

5 1/2 cups chicken stock or broth
1 1/4 pounds asparagus, cut into 1 1/2 inch lengths
3/4 cup dry white wine
2 tablespoons olive oil
1 yellow onion, chopped
2 cups Arborio rice
1 cup grated Parmesan cheese
1 tablespoon chopped fresh tarragon
salt and pepper to taste
fresh tarragon sprigs for garnish

In a saucepan over high heat, bring stock or broth to a boil. Add asparagus, boiling until just tender-crisp, 2 minutes. Using a slotted spoon, put vegetable into a bowl. Add wine to liquid and bring to a simmer. Be sure to keep liquid hot. In a large saucepan, warm the olive oil over medium-low heat. Add the onion and sauté until translucent, 8 minutes. Add the rice and stir about 1 minute. Add liquid slowly, keeping a simmer.

Cook, stirring constantly, until liquid is absorbed, about 2 minutes. Continue adding the liquid a little at a time, stirring constantly, until rice is just tender and the mixture is creamy, about 20–25 minutes longer. Add asparagus, cheese, and tarragon. Season with salt and pepper. Mix well. Spoon onto warmed plates and garnish with tarragon sprigs.

Cookies

Bel Air, Maryland

*To be rooted is perhaps the most important and
least recognized need of the human soul.*

—Simon Weil

Sherry Christmas Trees

Makes 2 dozen

I received this cookie recipe at an AAUW cookie exchange in San Jose in 1965. These cookies are made every Christmas.

1 1/2 cups un-sifted flour
1/2 cup white sugar
1/2 teaspoon salt
grated rind of 1 lemon
1/4 cup olive oil
1 egg
2 tablespoons sherry
green sugar
1 egg white

Mix all ingredients thoroughly, except green sugar and egg white. Roll out batter and cut cookies 1/8 inch thick using a Christmas tree cutter. Brush with beaten egg white; sprinkle tops with green sugar. Bake at 400 degrees for 8–10 minutes. Do not over bake.

Almond Oat Cookies

Makes 5 dozen

I made these for our sons and also took the recipe to AAUW cookie exchanges in San Jose in the mid-1960's.

    1 1/3 cups sugar
    1 1/3 cups butter
    6 cups quick cooking Quaker Oats
    2 eggs, beaten
    2 teaspoons almond extract
    2/3 cup slivered almonds

Cream sugar and butter together; mix in rolled oats. Add the beaten eggs, almond extract, and almonds, blending well. Mold into walnut-sized balls. Place on a greased baking sheet, and flatten to a ¼-inch thickness with a fork. Bake at 375 degrees for 10 minutes.

Cardamom Cookies

Makes 60

Cardamom is a popular spice in Swedish desserts, one I love.

    1 cup (2 sticks) unsalted butter
    1 cup powdered sugar
    1/2 cup granulated sugar
    1 large egg
    2 teaspoons vanilla
    2 1/4 cups flour
    1/2 teaspoon baking soda
    1 teaspoon black cardamom seeds

In a bowl, combine butter, sugars, egg, and vanilla. Beat until light and fluffy. Sift flour and baking soda into mixture, mixing well. Stir in cardamom seeds. Shape dough into two 10-inch logs the diameter of a quarter. Wrap logs in waxed paper and chill for at least an hour.

Preheat oven to 350 degrees. Cut logs into thin slices, 1/4-inch thick, and place on ungreased baking sheets. Bake for 10 minutes or until golden brown. Transfer the cookies to a wire rack. They burn easily.

Lavender and Lemon Zest Cookies

Makes 150 small cookies

I discovered these cookies at a Mozart chamber music concert.

- 1 cup (2 sticks) unsalted butter
- 1 cup confectioner's sugar
- 1/2 cup granulated sugar
- 1 large egg
- 2 teaspoons vanilla
- 2 1/4 cups flour
- 1/2 teaspoon baking soda
- 2 tablespoons lavender petals, finely chopped
- 2 tablespoons chopped lemon zest

In a large mixing bowl, combine butter, sugars, egg, and vanilla, and beat until light and fluffy. Sift the flour and baking soda into the mixture and mix well. Stir in the lavender petals and lemon zest. Shape the dough into three 6–8 inch long logs, just slightly bigger in circumference than a quarter. Wrap in waxed paper or parchment and refrigerate for at least an hour.

Preheat oven to 350 degrees. Cut the logs into very thin rounds, about 1/4 inch thick, and place them on ungreased baking sheets about 1 inch apart. Bake, watching very carefully, for about 10 minutes or until golden brown. Let the cookies cool for a few minutes on the baking sheet. Remove from sheet and cool completely.

Sand Dollars

Makes 3 dozen

An excellent, buttery cookie especially good with ice cream. This is a recipe our family has enjoyed since Kris was about three years old.

1 cup (2 sticks) unsalted butter
1 cup sugar
1 1/2 cups all-purpose flour
1/2 teaspoon baking soda
1 scant teaspoon salt
1/2 teaspoon distilled vinegar

Preheat oven to 350 degrees. Cream butter that is at room temperature and sugar together, and blend in the rest of the ingredients. Drop rounded teaspoons of dough, 2 inches apart, on an ungreased baking sheet and press into 2 1/2-3 inch rounds using a flat-bottomed glass dipped in water, then sugar. Bake for 12–15 minutes, until golden brown around the edges. Remove from baking sheet immediately. Cool on a rack.

Peanut Butter Cookies

Makes 4 dozen

I made these for my boys and now make them for my grandchildren. My mother made them for me as a child.

  1 cup (2 sticks) unsalted butter
  1 cup sugar
  1 cup brown sugar
  1 cup chunky peanut butter
  2 eggs, well beaten
  2 1/2 cups flour
  1/4 teaspoon baking soda
  pinch of salt
  1 teaspoon vanilla

Mix butter, sugars, and peanut butter and vanilla in a bowl. Cream thoroughly. Add eggs and mix well. Sift flour, baking soda, and salt into the mixture. Separate dough, roll into two logs, and put in wax paper or foil. (One roll may be frozen, if desired.) Preheat oven to 250 degrees. Cut cookies from roll. Let sit a short time; place on a lightly greased cookie sheet or on parchment paper on the sheet. Press down with a fork and bake for 12–15 minutes.

Gingersnaps I

Makes 2 dozen

This recipe is from Karl's pre-school in La Habra. He brought the cookies and the recipe home on Thanksgiving in 1968.

3/4 cup Crisco
1 cup sugar
4 tablespoons molasses
1 egg
2 cups flour
2 teaspoons baking soda
1/4 teaspoon salt
1 teaspoon cinnamon
3/4 teaspoon ginger
1 teaspoon cloves

Cream Crisco and sugar. Add molasses and egg, mixing well. Sift flour, soda, salt, and spices. Add to wet mixture, mixing well. Roll in balls the size of walnut. Dip balls in granulated sugar. Bake at 375 degrees for 15 minutes. Do not flatten.

Gingersnaps II

Makes 4 dozen

I first made these cookies from *Casual Occasions* in 1968.

1 cup (2 sticks) unsalted butter
1 1/4 cups sugar
1 extra-large egg
1/2 cup dark molasses
2 1/2 cups all-purpose flour
1 1/2 teaspoons baking soda
1/2 teaspoon salt
2 tablespoons ground ginger
2 tablespoons minced candied ginger
1 1/4 cups pecan halves, toasted and coarsely chopped

In a large bowl, combine butter and sugar. Using an electric mixer, beat until mixture is fluffy and light. Add egg, and continue to beat until fully incorporated; beat in molasses. In another bowl, sift together flour, baking soda, salt, and ground ginger. With mixer on low, beat flour mixture into the butter mixture, one-third at a time, beating well after each addition. Stir in candied ginger and pecans. Turn the dough out onto a lightly floured work surface. Knead briefly and divide into two equal portions. Using your palms, roll each dough portion into a log 1–1 1/2 inches wide. Wrap logs separately in plastic wrap, refrigerating until chilled, about 2 hours. Preheat oven to 325 degrees. Line two baking sheets with parchment paper. On a lightly floured work surface, slice dough logs crosswise 1/8 inch thick. Place dough rounds 1 inch apart on sheets. Bake until golden, 8–10 minutes.

Gingersnaps III

These gingersnaps are from Swedish chef Marcus Samuelsson of Aquavit. I have dined twice there, in New York and Minneapolis.

1/2 cup sugar
1/2 cup light brown sugar
1 cup (2 sticks) unsalted butter
1 egg
1/2 cup molasses
2 1/4 cups all-purpose flour
2 teaspoons ginger
1/2 teaspoon cloves
1/2 teaspoon cardamom
1/2 teaspoon cinnamon
2 teaspoons baking soda
1/2 teaspoon salt
1/2 teaspoon white pepper
1 cup candied orange peel, coarsely chopped
sugar for decoration

Preheat oven to 350 degrees. In a medium bowl, cream together sugars and butter until light and fluffy. Add egg and molasses, and combine thoroughly. In a separate bowl, sift together all dry ingredients. Combine with wet ingredients; then fold in the candied orange peel. Place dough in refrigerator until well chilled. Shape dough into 1-inch rounds. Roll in sugar and place 2 inches apart on parchment covered cookie sheet. Bake until golden brown, about 7 minutes. Remove to a rack and cool.

Three-Nut Cookies

Makes 2 dozen

This is a good old-fashioned cookie, especially if you like nuts.

1/2 cup all-purpose flour
1 teaspoon cream of tartar
1/2 teaspoon salt
1/2 teaspoon baking soda
1/2 cup (1 stick) unsalted butter
3/4 cup granulated sugar
1 egg
1/2 cup coarsely chopped almonds
1/2 cup coarsely chopped macadamia nuts
1 cup pecans, grated
1/2 cup brown sugar
1 tablespoon cinnamon

Preheat oven to 400 degrees. Grease two cookie sheets. Sift together flour, cream of tartar, baking soda, and salt. Set aside. In a large bowl, cream the butter and sugar until fluffy. Beat in the egg. Add dry ingredients to the wet mixture in two parts. Mix well. Stir in the coarsely chopped macadamia nuts, almonds and pecans. Thoroughly mix in the brown sugar, and cinnamon. Pinch off walnut-sized pieces of dough and form into balls. Roll each ball in the pecan sugar mixture and place on cookie sheets about 2 inches apart. Do not flatten. Bake about 10 minutes or until browned.

Gingerbread Men

Makes 1 dozen

Our sons loved decorating these cookies. When their friends visited before Christmas, each chose one from the tree to take home.

Cookies

    2 1/2 cups unbleached all-purpose flour
    1 1/2 teaspoons cinnamon
    1/2 teaspoon baking soda
    1/4 teaspoon cloves
    1 teaspoon salt
    3/4 cup (1 1/2 sticks) unsalted butter
    1/2 cup packed dark brown sugar
    1/2 cup light molasses
    1 large egg

Sift flour, ginger, cinnamon, baking soda, cloves, and salt in a medium bowl. Using electric mixer, beat butter, sugar, and molasses until fluffy. Add egg. Add dry ingredients, stirring. Gather dough into a ball (dough will be soft). Divide into 3 pieces; flatten each into a disk. Wrap in plastic and chill until firm, 1 hour. (May be made 1 day ahead.) Position rack in upper third of oven. Preheat to 375 degrees. Roll out 1 dough disk on floured surface to 1/4-inch thickness. Using a 5-inch cookie cutter, cut out gingerbread men. Transfer to parchment lined cookie sheets, spacing 1 inch apart. Gather scraps; chill. Bake cookies until just turning brown on edges, 10 minutes. Transfer to rack; cool. Repeat rolling, cutting, and baking with remaining dough.

Icing

3/4 cup confectioners' sugar
4 tablespoons milk

Mix sugar and milk. Spread on cookies as desired. Let stand for 30 minutes. Store cookies in airtight containers between sheets of waxed paper.

Pepper Sugar Cookies

Makes 4 dozen

I love these cookies and have made them through the years. The recipe is from Lee Bailey's 1991 *California Wine Country Cooking*. I have enjoyed all of his cookbooks.

    1 cup (2 sticks) unsalted butter, softened
    1 1/4 cups sugar, divided
    2 eggs
    1 teaspoon vanilla
    1/2 teaspoon salt
    1 teaspoon cream of tartar
    2 1/4 cups all-purpose flour
    1 tablespoon allspice
    1/2 teaspoon black pepper

Cream the butter and 1 cup of sugar until light and fluffy. Add the eggs one at a time, beating well. Add the vanilla and mix. Sift together the salt, cream of tartar, and flour, then add to the batter, beating until you have a semi-stiff dough. Refrigerate for 20 minutes. Meanwhile, preheat the oven to 350 degrees.

Mix the remaining 1/4 cup of sugar, allspice, and black pepper in a bowl and spread on a sheet of wax paper. Roll dough into balls by the spoonful; then roll in the spiced sugar to coat. Place on a cookie sheet, allowing space for them to expand.

Bake until lightly golden, about 10–12 minutes.

Spritz

Makes 4 dozen

Nana made this Swedish cookie every Christmas.

  1 cup (2 sticks) unsalted butter, softened
  3/4 cup sugar
  3 egg yolks, well beaten
  1 1/2 teaspoons pure vanilla
  2 1/2 cups all-purpose flour
  1/4 teaspoon salt
  1/2 teaspoon almond flavoring

Beat the butter and sugar until fluffy, 2–3 minutes. Add egg yolks, vanilla and almond flavoring, beating until incorporated. On low speed, gradually add the flour and salt. Chill batter.

Scrape dough into a cookie press that has been fitted with a decorative plate. Hold the cookie press perpendicular to the ungreased baking sheet with the tip almost touching the sheet, and squeeze the trigger. Continue to press out the cookies, spacing about 1 inch apart.

Preheat oven to 350 degrees. Bake cookies for about 6–9 minutes or just until the edges are barely tinged with brown. Remove from oven and gently transfer cookies to a wire rack to cool completely. These cookies will keep at room temperature for about 1 week or they may be frozen for several months.

Lindsay's Sugar Cookies

Makes 40

This recipe originally came from *Chez Panisse Desserts*. I found it in Suzanne Goin's *Sunday Suppers at Lucques* published in 2005. Karl introduced us to her Los Angeles area restaurant, Lucques.

1 cup (2 sticks) unsalted butter, softened
3/4 cup sugar, plus a little extra for rolling
1 large egg yolk
1 teaspoon pure vanilla
2 cups all-purpose flour
1/4 teaspoon Kosher salt
black pepper

Preheat oven to 350 degrees. Cream the butter at high speed, about 1 minute. Add the sugar and egg York, beating 3-4 minutes at medium high until light and fluffy. Slowly add the flour and salt, and mix at low speed until the dough comes together.

Shape the dough into logs about 1 1/2 inches in diameter. Roll the logs in sugar, then wrap in plastic and refrigerate until firm. Sprinkle with pepper and bake 10–12 minutes.

Renee's Lemon Bars

Makes 18

These bars are from *Nordstrom's Friends and Family Cookbook.*

Crust

> 1 cup (2 sticks) unsalted butter, softened
> 1 cup confectioners' sugar
> 2 cups all-purpose flour

Filling

> 4 large eggs
> 2 cups granulated sugar
> 1 tablespoon lemon zest, grated
> 6 tablespoons fresh lemon juice
> 1/3 cup all-purpose flour
> 1 teaspoon baking powder
> confectioners' sugar for dusting

Preheat the oven to 325 degrees. Butter a l9 x 13-inch baking pan.

Cream together the butter and confectioners' sugar until light. Add flour, mixing until well blended. Spread mixture on the bottom and up the sides of prepared pan.

Bake crust until lightly browned, 15–20 minutes. Remove from oven. Set on a wire rack to cool. Raise oven temperature to 350 degrees.

Beat the eggs until blended, 2 minutes. Add granulated sugar and beat until thick. Add lemon zest, lemon juice, flour, and baking powder, beating until well-blended and pale yellow. Pour filling over the baked crust, spreading it evenly with a rubber spatula.

Bake until filling is set—firm on edges, but soft in middle—for 15–20 minutes. Remove from oven. Set on a wire rack to cool slightly. Dust tops with powdered sugar. Cut into bars about 3 x 2 inches. Serve warm. May store in the refrigerator for up to 3 days.

Chocolate Chocolate Chip Cookies

Makes 24

Our grandchildren love chocolate chip cookies! Tollhouse cookies were our boys' favorite. This recipe is from *Splendid Settings, The Art + Craft of Entertaining*. This book, by Jane Korman, is undoubtedly my most beautiful cookbook.

1 (1 1/2 ounce) bag bittersweet chocolate chips
6 tablespoons unsalted butter
3 eggs
1 cup sugar
1/3 cup all-purpose flour
1/2 teaspoon baking powder
1 (11 1/2) ounce bag semisweet chocolate chips
1 cup walnuts, chopped

In a double boiler over hot water, melt the bittersweet chocolate chips and butter.

In a large bowl, beat the eggs and sugar with electric beater until thickened. Slowly stir in the chocolate mixture.

Mix together flour and baking powder. Add the flour mixture, a little at a time, to the chocolate mixture. Gently fold in the semisweet chocolate chips and walnuts.

Form two logs. Wrap logs tightly with plastic wrap. The dough will be very soft. Refrigerate for at least 1 hour until firm.

Preheat oven to 375 degrees. Grease two cookie sheets or line them with parchment paper. Unwrap the dough, and with a sharp knife, cut the logs into 3/4-inch slices. Place the slices 1 1/2 inches apart on the prepared cookie sheets. Bake for 12–14 minutes, or until a shiny crust forms on the tops of the cookies and the interiors are still soft.

Desserts

Fullerton, California

*Home is the centre and circumference, the start
and the finish, of most of our lives.*

—Charlotte Perkins Gilman

Lemon Meringue Pie

Serves 8

I remember my mother making this delicious pie in Fresno.

Crust

    1–1 1/4 cups graham cracker crumbs
    1/2 cup walnuts, chopped
    7 tablespoons unsalted butter, melted

Filling

    3 egg yolks
    1 (14-ounce) can sweetened condensed milk
    1/2 cup freshly squeezed lemon juice

Meringue

    3 egg whites
    1/8 teaspoon cream of tartar
    1/2 cup sugar

For Crust

Preheat oven to 350 degrees. In medium bowl, mix graham cracker crumbs, walnuts, and butter. Pour into a 9-inch pie plate. Press crumbs on bottom sides of plate. Bake at 350 degrees, 8–10 minutes, until set. Cool.

For Filling

Separate eggs. Combine milk, juice, and egg yolks. Pour into piecrust and refrigerate.

For Meringue

Combine egg whites with cream of tartar. Beat until foamy. Gradually add sugar, beating until stiff peaks form and sugar is dissolved. Increase oven temperature to 400 degrees. Drop meringue by teaspoons over lemon filling. Spread filling, making sure that meringue touches the crust on the pan edges. Make peaks and swirls in the meringue. Bake at 400 degrees, 10–15 minutes, or until meringue peaks start to brown. Cool on a wire rack for 30 minutes. Cover and refrigerate until serving.

Bananas Foster

Serves 6

I first made this dessert at our Adelaide Street duplex located off High Street in Oakland. Our view of the San Francisco Bay Bridge was spectacular. Erik celebrated his second birthday here.

1/2 cup (1 stick) unsalted butter
1/2 cup dark brown sugar, tightly packed
6 bananas, split in half lengthwise
6 ounces light or dark rum
heavy cream, chilled and whipped or vanilla ice cream

Melt butter and sugar slowly in a chafing dish. Add bananas, cooking 2 minutes on each side, until tender. Turn once. (They are easier to turn if you start bananas on round side.) Place bananas on individual plates. Add rum to chafing dish. Whisk and bring to slight boil. Ignite. Pour sauce over bananas. Serve with whipped cream or vanilla ice cream.

Dark Truffle Squares

Makes 64 pieces

I first made these for the installation service of Pastor Braatz at our church, Emanuel Lutheran Church, in La Habra in the mid-1980's.

   1/2 cup heavy cream, un-whipped
   1 tablespoon instant coffee
   8 tablespoons unsalted butter
   12 ounces semi-sweet chocolate, chopped

Line an 8 x 8-inch pan with foil. Set aside. Mix cream and coffee in a saucepan. Place over moderate heat and boil. Lower heat and add butter, stirring until blended. Remove from heat, adding chopped chocolate. Continue to stir until chocolate is completely melted and mixture thoroughly blended. Pour into foil-lined pan. Freeze until firm, 40 minutes or more. Invert onto a flat surface and remove foil. Cut truffles into 1-inch squares and dust with shaved chocolate. Place into small paper cups. Keep in refrigerator until serving.

Grasshopper Pie

Serves 6–8

This was served at my Alpha Omicron Pi sorority house at Cal and was one of the first desserts I made for Bob after we married.

Crust

24 Oreo chocolate cookies (2 cups)
4 tablespoons unsalted butter, melted

For Crust

Roll cookies finely. Add melted butter and blend. Line a 9-inch pie pan. Chill in refrigerator while preparing filling.

Filling

24 large marshmallows
2/3 cup milk
1/2 pint whipping cream
1/4 teaspoon peppermint extract
dash of green food coloring

For Filling

Melt marshmallows and milk in the top of a double boiler. Whip until smooth. Cool. Whip cream until stiff. Fold in peppermint and food coloring. Fold gently into cooled marshmallow mixture. Pour into pie shell and sprinkle a few crumbs on top. Chill overnight.

Dorothy's Angel Food Cake

Serves 10

This is excellent for a special birthday celebration! The recipe is from Dorothy Hagen, a friend from my working days at the Retired Senior Volunteer Program in Fullerton.

Cake

1 3/4 cups egg whites (10–12)
1 cup cake flour
1 1/2 cups sugar
2 teaspoons cream of tarter
1/2 teaspoon salt
1/4 teaspoon almond flavoring
1 teaspoon vanilla

Preheat oven to 325 degrees. Beat egg whites until they stand in peaks. Sift flour and sugar 7 times. When egg whites begin to foam, add cream of tartar and salt on medium low speed until foamy, about 1 minute. Gradually add sugar until soft, glossy peaks form, 1-2 minutes. Add vanilla and almond extract and beat until just blended. Fold in flour and beat for 2 minutes.

Gently scrape batter into a 16-cup tube pan with parchment paper but do not grease. Bake cake until golden brown and top springs back when pressed firmly, 50-60 minutes. Cool in pan for 1 1/2 hours. Run knife around edge of cake to loosen, then gently tap pan upside down on counter to release cake. Peel off parchment. Turn cake right side up on serving platter.

Frosting

1 (8-ounce) package cream cheese
1/4 pound unsalted butter
1 pound powdered sugar
3 teaspoons vanilla

Cream cheese and butter until fluffy. Add powdered sugar and vanilla, beating until good consistency for spreading.

Summer Berry Pie

Serves 8

Berkeley has wonderful berries for sale much of the year. The famous Monterey Market is a short walk for us. This recipe is from *The Cook's Illustrated Cookbook* and is a winner. The cookbook was a gift from Erik and Laura for Christmas 2013.

2 cups raspberries
2 cups blackberries
2 tablespoons red currant jelly
1/2 cup sugar
3 tablespoons cornstarch
1/2 teaspoon salt
1 tablespoon lemon juice

Graham cracker crust, baked. (A different crust recipe below.)

Gently toss berries together in a large bowl. Process 2 1/2 cups of berries in food processor until very smooth, about 1 minute. Strain purée through fine mesh strainer into small saucepan, pressing on solids to extract as much purée as possible. You should have about 1 1/2 cups. Discard solids. Whisk sugar, cornstarch, and salt together in bowl. Whisk mixture into strained purée. Bring purée mixture to a boil, stirring constantly and cook until it is as thick as pudding, about 7 minutes. Take off the stove and stir in lemon juice; set aside to cool slightly. Pour warm berry purée into pie shell. Melt jelly in small saucepan over low heat. Pour over remaining 3 1/2 cups berries and toss to coat. Spread berries evenly over purée and lightly press them into purée. Cover loosely with plastic wrap and refrigerate until filling is chilled and has set, about 3 hours. Serve chilled or at room temperature.

Rivoli Pumpkin Cheesecake

Serves 12–16

Rivoli on Solano is Berkeley's premier restaurant, and we have dined there for special occasions. I found this recipe in the *San Francisco Chronicle* and made it for a Thanksgiving in Portland.

Crust

1 1/2 cups gingersnaps, finely broken
1/2 cup pecans, toasted and ground
1/3 cup melted unsalted butter

Filling

1 1/2 pounds cream cheese
3/4 cup sugar
3 tablespoons cornstarch
1 1/2 teaspoons cinnamon
1 teaspoon ginger
pinch of nutmeg
pinch of salt
3/4 cup sour cream
1 1/2 cups puréed Kabocha squash (a Japanese squash similar to a sweet potato)
1/2 cup brown sugar, packed
1 tablespoon molasses
2 teaspoons vanilla
3 large eggs

Topping

1 1/2 cups sour cream

6 tablespoons sugar

For Crust

Preheat oven to 350 degrees. In a bowl, stir the gingersnaps and pecans. Add the butter and stir to blend. Press evenly onto the bottom and about 1/2 inch up the sides of a 10-inch spring-form pan. Bake 15 minutes. Remove and reduce oven temperature to 325 degrees.

For Filling

Beat cream cheese on low speed until smooth. In a bowl, stir together the sugar, cornstarch, cinnamon, ginger, nutmeg, and salt until well blended. Add to cream cheese and mix on low to medium speed until blended. Add sour cream and mix until blended. Add squash purée, brown sugar, molasses, and vanilla and mix until blended, scraping the bowl once or twice. Add the eggs one at a time, beating until blended. Pour batter into prepared crust, spreading evenly. Bake until mostly set, 50–60 minutes. Cool on a rack for 5 minutes.

For Topping

Whisk the topping ingredients and spread evenly over the cheesecake. Return to the oven for 5 minutes. Cool completely in the pan on a rack, then refrigerate overnight.

To serve, remove the outer cake pan ring. Cut into thin slices with a hot knife.

Nana's Apple Pie

Serves 6–8

Nana made this pie for Thanksgiving and Christmas dinners.

Crust

2 cups all-purpose flour
1/2-1 teaspoon salt
3/4 cup Crisco
2–6 tablespoons iced water

Filling

8 cups (8 medium) tart apples, diced in 1-inch pieces
1 cup sugar
1 teaspoon cinnamon
1/8 teaspoon salt
1 tablespoon lemon juice
1/2 teaspoon nutmeg
2 tablespoons butter

Mix flour and salt. Cut in Crisco until particles are size of small peas. Sprinkle with ice water, 1 tablespoon at a time, until all flour is moistened and pastry almost cleans side of bowl. Gather pastry

into a ball. Divide in half, shaping into 2 flattened rounds on a lightly floured surface. Wrap in plastic wrap. Refrigerate about 45 minutes until dough is firm, cold, and pliable.

Heat oven to 425 degrees. Roll one round 2 inches larger than upside-down 9-inch pie plate. Fold pastry into fourths; place in pie plate. Unfold and put into pie plate, pressing firmly against bottom and side.

Mix sugar, cinnamon, salt, lemon juice, and nutmeg. Stir in apples. Spoon into a pie plate. Cut butter into small pieces and sprinkle over filling. Trim overhanging edge of pastry 1/2 inch from rim of plate.

Roll other round of pastry into a 10-inch round. Fold into fourths and cut slits so steam can escape. Unfold top pastry over filling so the trim overhangs the edge one inch from rim of plate. Press rim to seal. Cover edge with 2–3-inch strip of foil to prevent excessive browning. Bake 40–50 minutes or until crust is brown and juice begins to bubble through slits in crust. Remove foil for the last 15 minutes of baking.

Serve with a scoop of vanilla ice cream, if desired.

Whipped Cream Pound Cake

A simple and delicious cake that is good plain or toasted.

1 1/2 cups sifted flour
1 cup sugar
2 teaspoons baking powder
1/2 teaspoon salt
1/2 pint heavy cream
2 eggs
1 teaspoon vanilla

Sift flour again with sugar, baking powder, and salt. Whip cream until stiff; beat in eggs and vanilla. Add sifted dry ingredients and stir until thoroughly blended. Pour batter into a buttered and sugar-dusted 2-quart loaf pan. Bake at 350 degrees for 55 minutes or until cake just begins to pull away from edge of pan. Let stand for 10 minutes. Turn out on a rack and let cool or serve warm.

Margarita Pie

Serves 6–8

This pie from the 1972 cookbook *Entertaining Is an Art* is addictive. There were never leftovers when I served it in Fullerton.

Crust

3/4 cup pretzel crumbs
3 tablespoons sugar
5 tablespoons butter, melted
2 tablespoons pretzel crumbs, for garnish

For Crust

Crush 3/4 cup pretzels. Combine crumbs and sugar. Add melted butter gradually, until blended. Press mixture firmly against bottom and sides of buttered 9-inch pie plate. Chill.

Filling

4 lemons (slice 1 lemon into thin slices for garnish)
1 envelope unflavored gelatin
4 egg yolks, beaten
1/2 cup sugar
7 tablespoons sugar
1/4 teaspoon salt
5 tablespoons tequila
3 tablespoons triple sec
5 egg whites

For Filling

Grate 1 teaspoon lemon rind from 3 lemons. Yields 7 tablespoons juice. Soften gelatin in lemon juice, 5 minutes. Beat egg yolks in top of double boiler. Blend in 1/2 cup sugar, salt, and rind. Add gelatin mixture. Over boiling water, stir constantly, until slightly thickened and gelatin thoroughly dissolved, 7 minutes. Transfer to bowl. Blend in liquors. Refrigerate, stirring frequently, until just cold to the touch. Beat egg whites to soft peaks. Gradually add 7 tablespoons sugar. Beat until all sugar is added and egg whites have soft peaks. Fold yolk mixture into whites. Spoon into chilled piecrust. Sprinkle with additional crumbs. Chill until firm.

Chart House Mud Pie

Serves 6

Bob and I loved this pie at the Chart House in Redondo Beach. When I made it at home, the plate wouldn't fit in our refrigerator so I had to freeze it in our neighbor Mrs. Wall's refrigerator.

1/2 package Nabisco chocolate wafers
1/2 cube butter, melted
1 quart coffee ice cream, softened
whipped cream and slivered toasted almonds for garnish

Crush wafers and add butter, mixing well. Press into a 10-inch pie plate. Cover with ice cream. Put in the freezer until ice cream is firm. Top with cold fudge sauce. Pie should stay in freezer over-night. Slice. Serve with whipped cream and slivered almonds.

Banana Cream Cracker Pie

Serves 6

I prepared this dessert at our Q Street apartment in Sacramento. When I opened the refrigerator, it slipped and fell face down on the kitchen floor. No dessert that night!

Crust

2 1/2 cups graham cracker crumbs
2/3 cup sugar
3/4 cup unsalted melted butter

For Crust

Mix crumbs, sugar, and butter together. Press mixture into bottom and sides of a 10-inch pie plate and bake for 6–8 minutes. Remove from oven and let cool.

Filling:

1 (8-ounce) package cream cheese
1 package vanilla pudding mix
1/2 cup whole milk
1/2 pint whipping cream
2 bananas

For Filling

Blend cream cheese with pudding mix. Add milk to pudding mixture. Pour into a prepared crust. Cool. When pudding is set, slice bananas on top. Cover with whipped cream and chill overnight.

A Master Pie Crust

Makes 2 crusts

Butter gives this forging crust its rich flavor.

   3 1/2 cups all-purpose flour
   1 cup (2 sticks) unsalted butter, chilled and cut into 1/2-inch cubes
   1/3 cup Crisco
   1 tablespoon 1 teaspoon sugar
   1 tablespoon Kosher salt
   1/4 cup ice water

Process flour, butter, Crisco, sugar, and salt in food processor until butter resembles tiny pebbles, 25 seconds. Transfer flour mixture to a bowl. Gradually add 1/4 cup ice water, stirring until dough is thoroughly combined. Press plastic wrap over surface of dough. Chill 1 hour or overnight.

Key Lime Pie

Serves 8

Whenever I enjoy this pie, memories return of Karl and I sharing a piece in Fernandina Beach, Florida. Bob, Kris, and I visited him in Gainesville in 1989 for Thanksgiving. He received his master's degree in Creative Writing, studying under America's poet laureate Donald Justice at the University of Florida.

Crust

2 cups graham cracker crumbs
1/2 cup granulated sugar
1/2 cup melted unsalted butter

Filling

8 egg yolks
2 (14-ounce) cans sweetened condensed milk
1 1/2 cups Key lime juice
grated rind and zest of 2 Key limes
sweetened whipped cream

For Crust

Preheat oven to 350 degrees. Mix crumbs, sugar, and melted butter until blended. Press into bottom and sides of a 9-inch or 10-inch pie plate and bake for 60 minutes. Remove from oven and chill for 15 minutes.

For Filling

Beat egg yolks with condensed milk. While stirring, add the Key lime juice. Add the grated Key lime rind and zest. Pour mixture into the chilled crust. Bake for 8–10 minutes

Chill several hours before serving. Slice pie and top with a dollop of sweetened whipping cream. Garnish with lime slices. Serve immediately.

Chocolate Mousse Torte with Cold Zabaglione Sauce

Serves 10

This dessert is one of the best I've ever tasted.

Filling

8 ounces bittersweet chocolate
1 cup unsalted butter
1 cup sugar
1/4 cup brewed coffee
10 eggs, separated
1 teaspoon vanilla
1/2 cup flour
1/2 teaspoon salt

Zabaglione

1 cup dry Marsala wine
7 egg yolks
7 tablespoons sugar
1 cup heavy whipping cream
2 cups raspberries or strawberries

Preheat oven to 350 degrees. Butter bottom and sides of a 9-inch spring-form pan. Line bottom of pan with parchment paper.

For Filling

In the top pan of a double boiler, combine chocolate, butter, sugar and coffee. Heat until chocolate and butter are melted. Stir until smooth.

Remove from heat and whisk in egg yolks and vanilla. Then fold in the flour and salt.

Using an electric mixer, set on medium speed, beat egg whites until frothy. Increase speed to high beating until medium firm peaks form. Gently fold egg whites into the batter just until they fully disappear. Do not over mix. Transfer batter to prepared pan. Bake the torte until it springs back when touched lightly in the center, 45–60 minutes.

For Zabaglione

While the torte is baking, make the zabaglione. In a bowl, whisk together the Marsala, egg yolks, and sugar until well blended. Pour through a fine-mesh sieve into the top pan of a large double boiler. Place the pan over simmering water. Using a whisk or an electric mixer set on medium, beat until thickened, pale and fluffy, 10–15 minutes. The mixture should double in volume.

Remove the pan from heat and immediately nest in a bowl of ice to cool it down completely. In a chilled bowl with chilled beaters, whip the cream until stiff peaks form. Fold the cold custard into the whipped cream. Cover and refrigerate.

Remove the torte from the oven when done and let cool completely in the pan on a wire rack. Remove the pan sides and transfer the torte to a serving plate. Cut into wedges and serve with the zabaglione sauce and the berries.

Profiteroles

Serves 12 for dessert or 36 for tiny portions.

These cream puffs make a memorable finale to a special dinner.

1/2 cup butter
2/3 cup hot water
1 cup flour
1/2 teaspoon salt
4 eggs
ice cream or whipped cream

Bring butter and water to a boil in a saucepan. Remove from heat and add flour and salt all at once. Cook over medium heat, stirring constantly until mixture leaves side of pan and forms a stiff ball. Add eggs one at a time, beating well after each addition. (May cover and store dough in refrigerator for up to 3 days.) Drop into 12 mounds

3-4 inches apart on nonstick baking sheet, or add parchment to baking sheet. (Dough may be dropped into 36 small mounds for bite size puffs.) Bake at 450 degrees for 5 minutes. Reduce oven temperature to 350 degrees. Continue baking for 15 minutes or until golden brown. Turn off oven. Prick puffs with sharp knife to allow steam to escape. Let stand in oven for 20 minutes. Split puffs into halves horizontally. Fill each half with ice cream or fill one half and top with the other half and cover with hot fudge sauce. Note: baked profiteroles may be frozen, thawed, and heated in a 350 degree oven for 10–15 minutes or until crisp.

Swedish Cream with Raspberry Sauce

Serves 8

I served this in 2002 for Stig-Eyrik and Mimi, my cousins from Finland. The recipe is from the *Timberline Lodge Cookbook*.

Swedish Cream

2 cups heavy cream
3/4 cup sugar
1 tablespoon vanilla
1 tablespoon unflavored Knox gelatin
3 cups sour cream
raspberry sauce

Raspberry Sauce

2 cups raspberries
lemon juice

Simple Syrup

3 tablespoons sugar
2 tablespoons water

For Swedish Cream

Combine the cream, sugar, vanilla, and unflavored gelatin in a saucepan. Heat until hot but not boiling. Remove from heat and stir in sour cream. Pour into serving dishes, and chill until set about 3 hours. Prepare the Raspberry Sauce and mix with the Swedish Cream. Chill for at least 3 hours.

For Raspberry Sauce (and Simple Syrup)

Purée the raspberries in a blender or food processor. Push the purée through a sieve using a rubber spatula to remove all the seeds. Bring the sugar and water to a boil in a small saucepan to make the simple syrup. Add the simple syrup to the strained purée and blend together. Add lemon juice to taste.

Tiramisu

Serves 8

This is an elegant dessert to end a memorable meal of butterflied leg of lamb with juniper berries and rosemary. (See Meats)

> 6 egg yolks
> 1 cup sugar
> 1/2 cup sweet Marsala wine
> 3 (8-ounce) packages cream cheese, cut into pieces
> 1 1/2 cups brewed espresso, at room temperature
> 1/2 cup Kahlua liqueur
> 1–2 packages ladyfingers
> 1 cup sweetened heavy cream for garnish
> shaved semisweet chocolate for garnish

Mix egg yolks and sugar until fluffy. Add Marsala wine and mix. Slowly add cream cheese until mixture is thick and creamy.

Combine espresso and Kahlua, and quickly dip the ladyfingers, one at a time, into this mixture. Line 8 individual glass dishes or wine goblets with ladyfingers, and spoon in cream cheese mixture. Refrigerate until ready to serve. Just before serving, add a dollop of whipping cream topped with a small portion of the shaved chocolate for garnish.

Graham Cracker Pound Cake

This recipe is from Chef Megan Garretts of Bluestem in Kansas City, Missouri. Bob and I had the pleasure of eating at this 5-star restaurant on an Art Guild trip in 2006.

    vegetable oil spray
    1 1/2 sticks unsalted butter, softened
    1/2 cup granulated sugar
    1/4 cup dark brown sugar
    1 1/2 cups cake flour
    1/2 cup graham crackers crumbs, finely ground
    1/4 teaspoon baking powder
    1/4 teaspoon salt
    3 tablespoons whole milk
    2 tablespoons heavy cream
    3 large eggs
    1 tablespoon vanilla

Preheat oven to 325 degrees. Spray an 8 x 4-inch glass loaf pan with vegetable oil spray. In a large bowl, using an electric mixer, cream butter with granulated and dark brown sugars. In a medium bowl, whisk cake flour with graham cracker crumbs, baking powder, and salt. In a small bowl, whisk together the milk, cream, eggs, and vanilla. Beating at medium speed, add dry and liquid ingredients to the butter mixture in three alternating batches.

Scrape the batter into the prepared loaf pan, and bake in the lower third of the oven for about 55 minutes, until a toothpick inserted in the center comes out with a few moist crumbs attached. Let cool in the pan for 15 minutes; turn pound cake onto a rack to cool completely. May be kept in an airtight container for 3 days or frozen for 2 weeks.

Princess Cake

Serves 12–14

This was the unique dessert on the menu of the one-of-a-kind restaurant, Gustav Anders in Costa Mesa. Laura and I split a piece there once. In Sweden, it is baked for birthdays and weddings.

Cake

8 eggs, separated
1 cup sugar
2 1/2 cups flour
1/2 teaspoon baking powder
3 ounces butter, melted
1/2 teaspoon salt
8 ounces raspberry jam

Cream Filling

2 cups half & half
5 egg yolks
3 tablespoons cornstarch
1/2 cup sugar
pinch of salt
1 teaspoon vanilla
4 tablespoons cold unsalted butter, cut into small pieces

Whipped Cream

3 cups heavy cream
3 tablespoons sugar
1 tablespoon vanilla

Simple Syrup

1 cup sugar
1 cup water

For Marzipan

1/2 pound store-bought marzipan

Marzipan Dome

1 1/2 pounds confectioners' sugar
3 drops green food coloring for rolling the marzipan

For Cake

Whip egg yolks until pale yellow and doubled in volume. In another bowl, whip egg whites until frothy, gradually adding sugar until the foam becomes stiff. Fold half of the whipped egg whites in the yolks. Fold in remaining egg whites thoroughly, until uniform in color. In four batches, fold in sifted flour and baking powder; then butter.

Immediately pour the batter into two 10-inch greased cake pans, and bake in a preheated 350-degree oven for about 30 minutes or until a toothpick inserted in the middle comes out clean. Allow the cakes to cool on a rack. After they've cooled, run the tip of a knife around the edge of the cakes to loosen them from the pans and remove. Using a long serrated knife, slice both the cakes into 12 thick disks. Only 3 will be needed.

For Cream Filling

Bring the milk and vanilla bean to a simmer in a medium saucepan; Remove from heat and let sit for 10 minutes to infuse. Whisk the eggs, cornstarch, sugar, and salt in a bowl until smooth. Add half of the milk into the bowl containing the eggs, whisking constantly; return the mixture to the saucepan containing the remaining milk. Whisk over moderate heat.

Continue whisking until the mixture is thickened and begins to simmer. Allow cream filling to simmer, whisking for an additional 2 minutes. Transfer into another bowl. Cover and allow to cool completely.

For Whipped Cream

Whisk heavy cream with sugar and vanilla until firm and holds its shape. Do not over whip.

For Simple Syrup

Bring water and sugar to a boil. Remove from heat and allow to cool.

For Marzipan

Color a walnut-sized piece of marzipan with green food coloring until deep green. Reserve. Using a fine mesh strainer, dust a clean work surface with confectioners' sugar. Tear off a pea-sized piece of green marzipan and knead it with the remaining marzipan until uniform in color. Add additional pieces from green marzipan until it achieves a light green color (the color of a Granny Smith apple). Discard the leftover deep green marzipan.

To Assemble

Place a 10-inch spring form pan without a bottom on a 12-inch cake board. Place one layer of the sponge cake on the bottom, and generously brush with the syrup. Spread the jam evenly over the syrup and place a second layer of sponge cake on top of the jam. Brush with syrup and spread the prepared cream on this layer. Top with a third layer of sponge cake and again, brush with syrup. Using your hand, press lightly on the cake to ensure cake is level. Refrigerate for 1 hour.

Remove the cake from the spring form mold and generously frost the sides with the reserved whipped cream. Pour the remaining whipped cream directly on the center of the top of the cake and using a spatula, make a mound, working from the center out. The height of the whipped cream should be approximately 1 1/2 inches in the center and about 1/2 inch on the edges.

Dust a work surface again with confectioners' sugar and roll the light green marzipan into one 10-inch thick circle, using as much confectioner's sugar as necessary during rolling to prevent the marzipan from sticking to the work surface. When finished rolling, the marzipan should form a 18-inch circle of even thickness. This should be enough to cover the entire cake and sides. Gently lay it down on top of the cake, smoothing out the dome. Dust the entire cake with confectioner's sugar.

Poppy Seed Cake

Serves 8–10

The recipe for this cake (similar to a pound cake) was given to me in 1990 by a fellow docent, Mel Hyde, during my years with the outstanding docent program of the Art Alliance at CSUF.

 1 package yellow cake mix
 4 eggs
 1 large package Jell-O instant vanilla pudding mix
 1/2 cup vegetable oil
 1/4 cup poppy seeds
 2 teaspoons vanilla, to taste
 1 cup water

Mix ingredients and beat 10 minutes. Pour into a bundt pan. Bake at 350 degrees for 50–60 minutes. While still warm, sift confectioner's sugar over the top.

Bonne Orange

Serves 8

I first made this recipe from a 1980 *Gourmet* for a Mother's Day brunch in our Fullerton backyard by the pool.

    1 (8-ounce) package and 1 (3-ounce) package cream cheese
    1/3 cup sugar
    1/8 teaspoon salt
    16-ounce can concentrated orange juice, thawed and undiluted
    2 teaspoons vanilla
    1 1/2 cups heavy cream, whipped
    a graham cracker crust
    1 orange, peeled and sectioned
    mint leaves for garnish
    candied violets for garnish

Mix cream cheese, sugar, and salt with electric mixer, beating until smooth. Blend in orange juice and vanilla. Gently fold in whipped cream. Spoon into graham cracker crust. Refrigerate overnight. Garnish with orange sections, mint, and candied violets.

Lemon Sour Cream Pie

Serves 8

Bob and I first enjoyed this pie in 1963 with Barbara and Butch in Berkeley. Bob's cousins were godparents to Karl.

1 cup sugar
3 tablespoons cornstarch
dash of salt
1 cup whole milk
3 eggs, separated
4 tablespoons butter, softened
1 teaspoon grated lemon peel
1/4 cup lemon juice
1 cup sour cream
1/4 teaspoon cream of tartar
1/2 teaspoon vanilla
6 tablespoons sugar
1 baked 9-inch pie shell

In a saucepan, combine sugar, cornstarch, and salt. Stir in milk, bringing to a boil. Cook until thick. Blend small amount of hot mixture into slightly beaten egg yolks. Return to stove, adding butter, lemon peel, and juice. Melt butter. Cover and cool. Fold in sour cream. Spoon into pie shell. Beat egg whites, cream of tartar, and vanilla until soft peaks form. Add sugar, beating until stiff. Spread on top of pie, sealing edges. Bake at 350 degrees for 12–15 minutes or until golden. Cool before serving.

Dulce de Leche Ice Cream Pie

Serves 8

Chocolate, caramel, and nuts in desserts and candy bars were popular in 2012. Toni, Laura, and I especially like the combination.

1 cup crushed graham cracker crumbs
1/2 stick (4 tablespoons) unsalted butter
1/4 teaspoon cinnamon
pinch of nutmeg
1 1/2 pints dulce de leche ice cream
1 1/2 cups Spanish peanuts, with skin on
peanut oil or canola oil for tossing with peanuts
sea salt
1 jar hot fudge sauce
½ cup cajeta (a Mexican caramel sauce)

Mix cracker crumbs with butter, cinnamon, and nutmeg in a medium bowl. Press crumbs into a 9-inch glass or ceramic pie plate. Bake crust for about 8 minutes or until firm to the touch. Remove crust from the oven and set aside to cool.

Remove ice cream from freezer and thaw at room temperature for 15–20 minutes, until slightly softened.

Spread peanuts on a baking sheet, toasting for 8–10 minutes and shaking the pan occasionally for even toasting. Remove nuts, drizzle with oil, sprinkle them with sea salt, and toss to coat.

Scoop ice cream into a bowl and beat until very soft, but not melted. Spread softened ice cream into cooled pie shell and freeze it while preparing rest of the components.

Warm hot fudge sauce and cajeta (caramel) sauce separately in a microwave oven.

When ready to serve, cut pie into wedges and place on plates. Place three small bowls of sauces and peanuts on the table for people to choose what they would like.

Cream Cheese Pastry Dough

A double crust pie

This recipe is from *Gourmet's* November 2003 issue and is adapted from a 1984 recipe.

3/4 cup (1 1/2 sticks) unsalted butter, softened
8 ounces cream cheese, softened
3 tablespoons sugar
1 teaspoon vanilla
pinch of salt
2 1/2 cups all-purpose flour

Beat butter, cream cheese, sugar, vanilla, and a pinch of salt in a bowl until fluffy, 1–2 minutes. Reduce speed to low. Add flour and mix until just combined.

Turn out dough onto a lightly floured surface and form into two balls, one slightly larger than the other. Flatten each into a 5–6 inch disk. Wrap disks separately in plastic wrap and chill until firm, at least 1 hour.

Cheesecake

Serves 6

Cheesecake became one of my favorite desserts during college.

    3 (3-ounce) packages cream cheese
    1/2 cup sugar
    2 eggs
    1/4 teaspoon vanilla
    dash of salt
    1 pint sour cream
    3 tablespoons sugar
    graham cracker crust

Cream the cream cheese, sugar, salt, and eggs, one at a time. Add vanilla. Mix well. Pour mixture into a graham cracker crust and bake 25 minutes or less. Cool for 10 minutes. Mix sour cream with 3 tablespoons sugar and spread over pie. Bake 5 minutes at 325 degrees. Chill for 24 hours.

Blum's Coffee Crunch Dessert

Serves 10

Blum's was an elegant restaurant popular in the 1950's in San Francisco.

Coffee Crunch

> vegetable oil to grease the baking sheet
> 1 1/2 cups sugar
> 1/4 cup strong coffee
> 1/4 cup light corn syrup
> 1 tablespoon baking soda, sifted after measuring

Grease baking sheet. Combine sugar, coffee, and corn syrup in a 4-quart saucepan and bring to a boil. (The mixture becomes foamy after baking soda is added and rises high in the pan.) Cook at 285 degrees on a candy thermometer, 6–7 minutes. Mixture will be smoky.

Remove pan from heat. Sprinkle baking soda on mixture. Mixture is hot and will foam up high. When it stops rising and foaming (1–2 minutes), immediately pour it onto the baking sheet. Spread mixture out with a spatula. Let sit until it has cooled and hardened.

Break coffee crunch into irregular (1/4–1/2-inch pieces). Store in an airtight container until ready to use. May be made two days ahead.

Cake

> , 8 large egg whites
> 1 1/2 cups sugar, divided
> 2 1/4 cups cake flour
> 1 tablespoon baking powder
> 1 teaspoon salt

1/2 cup vegetable oil
6 large egg yolks
3/4 cup water
2 teaspoons lemon zest, grated
1 tablespoon vanilla

For Cake

Preheat oven to 350 degrees. Using a portable electric mixer, beat the egg whites in a large mixing bowl until they begin to foam. Slowly add 3/4 cup of the sugar, and continue beating until the whites are stiff but still moist. Transfer to a bowl and set aside. Sift together flour, the remaining 3/4 cup sugar, baking powder, and salt in a small mixing bowl. Place the oil, egg yolks, 3/4 cup water, lemon zest, and vanilla in a large bowl, and beat with mixer until completely smooth. Add the flour mixture and stir to combine well. Gently fold 1/3 of the beaten egg whites into the batter. Once incorporated, drop the remaining whites onto the batter and fold them in. Pour the batter into an ungreased 10-inch tube pan, and smooth the top with a rubber spatula.

Bake in top half of oven 80–90 minutes, or until a wooden skewer inserted in the cake is clean. Remove from oven and immediately invert the pan onto neck of a wine bottle until it is completely cool. Turn pan right side up and use a knife to go around the side of the pan to loosen the cake. Push center up and remove cake from the pan. When done, wrap in plastic wrap until ready to frost. It will keep a day.

Frosting

3 cups (approximately (1 1/2 pints) heavy whipping cream
2 teaspoons vanilla
1/2 cup confectioner's sugar
1 tablespoon instant coffee

For Frosting

Combine the cream and vanilla in a deep bowl. Sift the powdered sugar and instant coffee together twice, and then add to the cream and vanilla. Using a whisk, rotary, or electric beater, whip the cream until soft peaks form. It must be stiff enough to spread.

To Assemble

Split the cake into two equal layers. Using a spatula, frost the bottom layer and sprinkle it with the coffee crunch. Place the second cake layer on top, frost it, and sprinkle the top and the sides of the cake generously with the coffee crunch.

Double Decker Pumpkin Ice Cream Pie

Serves 6

·

This has been a popular dessert at many Thanksgivings since 1963.

Crust

1 1/2 cups finely crushed graham cracker crumbs
1/3 cup sugar
1/3–1/2 cups unsalted butter, melted

Filling

1 pint vanilla ice cream
1 cup canned pumpkin
3/4 cup sugar
1/2 teaspoon nutmeg
1/2 teaspoon ginger
1/2 teaspoon cinnamon
1/2 teaspoon salt
1/2 pint heavy whipping cream

For Crust

Combine crumbs with sugar, and blend in melted butter. Press firmly onto bottom and sides of a 9-inch pie pan. Chill for 1 hour, or bake at 350 degrees for about 10 minutes to set crust. The baked crust will be firmer than a purchased crust.

For Filling

Line the pie shell with ice cream (allow it to soften slightly), making a layer about 1/2 inch thick. Place in the freezer while preparing the pumpkin layer. Blend together the pumpkin, sugar, nutmeg, ginger, cinnamon, and salt. Whip cream until stiff and fold into mixture. Spoon the filling over the ice cream lined pie shell. Return to freezer for at least 2 hours. To serve, remove from freezer and let stand at room temperature for 5 minutes. Slice into pieces.

Graham Cracker Crust for Summer Berry Pie

Makes 1 (9-inch) pie crust

This graham cracker crust recipe may be used in all recipes calling for this type of crust.

    8 whole Keebler graham crackers, broken into 1-inch pieces
    5 tablespoons unsalted butter, melted and cooled
    3 tablespoons sugar

Adjust oven rack to middle position and heat oven to 325 degrees. Process graham cracker pieces in a food processor to fine, even crumbs, 30 seconds. Sprinkle melted butter and sugar over crumbs and pulse to incorporate, about three pulses. Sprinkle mixture into a 9-inch pie plate. Using bottom of a measuring cup, press crumbs into even layer on bottom and sides of pie plate. Bake until crust begins to brown, 13–18 minutes. Transfer to a wire rack and cool completely.

Russian Tea Room Cheesecake

Serves 10

This New York City restaurant near Central Park has unfortunately closed. I was fortunate to go there twice, once with Bob and once with an Art Alliance friend, Toni Henley. This dessert differs from traditional creamy and dense cheesecakes by being very light.

 2 1/2 (8-ounce) packages cream cheese
 1 cup plus 2 tablespoons unsalted butter, softened
 additional butter for pan
 1 1/2 cups sugar, divided
 8 large eggs, separated
 2 teaspoons lemon zest, finely grated
 2 tablespoons fresh lemon juice
 1 teaspoon vanilla
 1/2 teaspoon orange flower water
 1/2 teaspoon almond extract
 1/4 cup cornstarch

Preheat oven to 350 degrees. Butter bottom and sides of a spring form pan. Line bottom with a round of parchment and butter round. Butter one side of parchment strip and fit other side of strip against buttered side of pan. Strip will extend 2 inches above rim of pan.

Beat together cream cheese, butter, 1 1/4 cup sugar, egg yolks, lemon zest, lemon juice, vanilla, orange flower water, and almond extract in a large bowl with an electric mixer at medium speed until creamy, about 3 minutes. Add cornstarch and mix at low speed until just combined.

Beat egg whites in another large bowl at medium speed until whites hold soft peaks. Add remaining 1/4 cup sugar, 1 tablespoon at a time, beating until meringue holds stiff, glossy peaks, about 3 minutes. Fold 1/4 of whites into cream cheese mixture to lighten; then fold in remaining whites gently, but thoroughly. Increase speed to high, and continue beating until meringue holds stiff, glossy peaks, about 3 minutes. Fold 1/4 of whites into cream cheese mixture. Fold in remaining whites gently but thoroughly.

Line outside of spring form pan with foil, covering bottom and about 1 inch up side to waterproof. Pour batter into pan and gently smooth top. Bake in a hot water bath in middle of oven until top is golden but cake trembles slightly when pan is gently shaken, 55–65 minutes. (Cheesecake will rise in oven, but will fall slightly and set as it cools.) Transfer spring form pan to a rack to cool completely. Chill at least 8 hours.

Note: Cheesecake may be chilled, covered, up to 3 days. To cut, use a thin sharp knife dipped into a tall glass of hot water.

Marion Cunningham's Coffeecake

Serves 8–10

Cakes such as this one have been popular for fifty years or more. I can remember Gaby baking something like it in San Leandro.

2 sticks unsalted butter, room temperature
1 cup sugar
3 eggs
2 1/2 cups all-purpose flour
2 teaspoons baking powder
1 teaspoon salt
1 cup sour cream
5 teaspoons vanilla extract

Preheat oven to 350 degrees. Grease and flour a 10-inch bundt pan. Put butter in a mixing bowl. Beat several seconds. Add sugar and beat until smooth. Add eggs, beating for 2 minutes, or until light and creamy. In a separate bowl mix flour, baking powder, baking soda, and salt; stir with a fork to blend. Add flour mixture to butter mixture, beating until smooth. Add sour cream and vanilla and mix.

Spoon batter into pan. Bake for 50 minutes, or until a straw is clean when inserted into the center. Remove from the oven and let rest for 5 minutes. Invert onto a rack and cool a little before slicing. Serve warm.

Peppered Balsamic Ice Cream
with Fresh Strawberries

Serves 4

This unique ice cream dessert is from Nancy Silverton's 2007 cookbook *A Twist of the Wrist*.

    1 pint premium vanilla ice cream
    1/2 teaspoon freshly ground black pepper
    2 tablespoons aged balsamic vinegar
    1 quart ripe strawberries
    1/2 cup sugar

Scoop ice cream into a large bowl, keeping carton to refreeze ice cream. Mix gently; add pepper, then the balsamic vinegar in a thin, steady stream, taking care not to let it splatter. Continue to mix for 10 minutes to incorporate the ingredients. (It's okay if the vinegar appears slightly streaky in the ice cream.) Spoon the ice cream back into the carton and refreeze for 45 minutes to 1 hour.

About 20 minutes before serving, cut strawberries in half and toss in a bowl with the sugar. Put 1 scoop of ice cream into each of four dessert dishes. Divide berries over dishes. Drizzle with vinegar.

Kokkari Flourless Chocolate Cake

Serves 12–16

Bob and I dined at Kokkari in the early 2000's, between Christmas and New Year, with Erik and Laura, Karl, and Kris and Toni. I have enjoyed lunches at this San Francisco restaurant many times with Janet. Bob and I first became acquainted with Greek cuisine when we hosted a Greek dinner in Maryland.

10 ounces (2 1/2 sticks) unsalted butter
10 ounces bittersweet chocolate, a minimum 70 percent cocoa
8 large eggs
1/2 teaspoon sea salt
2 tablespoons confectioners' sugar
2 tablespoons brewed coffee or espresso
2 tablespoons Metaxa
boiling water as needed
1 1/2 teaspoons unsweetened cocoa powder
heavy cream sweetened and whipped for garnish

Preheat oven to 350 degrees and set a rack in the middle of the oven. Lightly coat the bottom of a 9 x 3-inch round spring form pan with nonstick baking spray. Line the bottom with a round of parchment paper. Wrap the outside bottom of the spring form pan with a double thickness of aluminum foil to prevent leakage.

Put butter in the top of a double boiler and set over barely simmering water; the double boiler top should not touch the water. When butter is about half melted, stir in the chocolate. When the chocolate is about three-quarters melted, remove the double boiler from the stove. Stir gently until the mixture is melted and smooth. Set aside and cool to room temperature, about 20 minutes.

In a food processor, beat eggs and salt at medium-high speed until well blended. With processor running, add sugar, and beat until mixture is doubled in volume and pale yellow, 8–10 minutes. With a large spatula, incorporate melted chocolate and butter until thoroughly blended. Fold in coffee and brandy. Batter will be thin.

Pour batter into the prepared spring form pan and place pan inside a larger roasting pan. Add boiling water to come halfway up the side of the spring form pan. Bake until the cake feels firm on top, the edges beginning to pull away from the sides of the pan, and a skewer inserted into the center coming out with moist crumbs attached, about 1 hour and 15 minutes. (It is okay if the cake has begun to crack on top.) Remove the cake pan from the water bath, carefully discarding the foil, and place on a wire rack. Let the cake cool in the pan on the rack for 2 hours. The cake will sink slightly as it cools. Cover the pan with plastic wrap and let stand at room temperature until completely set, at least 6 hours or up to overnight.

To remove cake from the pan, run a sharp knife around the edge of the cake and release the spring form. Remove the pan sides and carefully use a large spatula to lift the cake. Peel parchment from the bottom and transfer the cake onto a serving platter. Alternatively, transfer the cake to a platter with the parchment. Remove parchment as you slice and serve the cake.

Before serving, put cocoa powder in a small sieve and sift evenly over cake surface. Repeat with confectioners' sugar. Cut into thin wedges and add a dollop of whipping cream.

About the Author

Connie Erickson Rosenquist began working on the cookbook *Remembrances, Residences, Recipes, and a Family Tree* over five years ago. In the 1970's and 1980's she enjoyed gourmet dinner groups in Fullerton, California and Bel Air, Maryland. At these monthly gatherings, the hostess would choose a country or theme and plan the menu. She prepared the entrée, purchased the beverages to be served, and assigned the other items including salad, vegetable, and dessert to others in the group. Two of the countries featured by Connie when she hosted were Greece and India.

Always interested in food preparation, Connie loved serving on a committee that prepared and published *After Five with Children's League: A Gourmet's Guide to Serving Delectable Hors d' oeuvres* in 1977. The proceeds of the book were used for further operation and expansion of the Children's Center Complex and to benefit youth activities in Fullerton. Connie and other members, all volunteers, shared some of their favorite recipes. A friend and fellow member, Dottie Gigliotti, provided sketches.

In 2004, Connie selected poems written by her and her husband Bob's son, Karl Robert, and had a book published posthumously with iUniverse. This tribute is entitled *Awake Unto Me.* Dr. Rosenquist received a BA degree from Northwestern University, a MA from the University of Florida and a PhD from UCLA. A professor of English at Santiago Canyon College in Orange, California. Karl died tragically and unexpectedly of a diabetic hypoglycemic reaction in July 2003.

Index

Beverages

Breads

Breakfast and Brunch

Cookies

Desserts

Fish

Meat

Sandwiches

Soups

3 Proverbs

Food must feast the eyes as well as the stomach.

—a Japanese proverb

*To invite anyone to dine implies that we charge ourselves
with his happiness all the time he is under our roof.*

—a French proverb

Reading and eating should both be done slowly.

—a Spanish proverb

Photos of Residences

Appetizers -   Monterey Avenue, Berkeley, California
Bob's childhood home 1940–1960 (our marriage)

Monterey Avenue, Berkeley, California
Our home from 1996–the present

Beverages -   605 West Laurel Lane, Visalia, California
Connie's childhood home 1950–1960 (our marriage)

Sherwood Drive, Cambria, California
Roy and Celia's home on the ocean

Breakfasts -   Tully Road near Jack Tone Road, Lodi, California
Roy's childhood home until 1932 (his marriage)

Breads -   Bradley, Hames Valley, California
Ina's childhood home until 1834 (her marriage)

Sandwiches -   2012 Grant Street, Berkeley, California
Celia's childhood home until 1932 (her marriage)

Soup -   1361 Santa Avenue, Berkeley, California
Harold's childhood home until 1934 (his marriage)

Salads -   Rodney Drive, San Leandro, California
Connie's childhood home 1940–1943

Poultry -   1552 Adoline Avenue, Fresno, California
Connie's childhood home 1943–1950

Meat -   274 San Antonio Way, Sacramento, California
             Our first home 1961–1962 (no picture available)

Fish -   2610 Thrasher Lane, San Jose, California
             Our home 1963–1966

Pasta -   801 Carlson Drive, Brea, California
             Our home 1966–1969

Cookies -   320 Linwood Avenue, Bel Air, Maryland
             Our home 1969–1973

Desserts - 3800 Rosehedge Drive, Fullerton, California
             Our home 1973–1995

Family Tree

Connie Leigh Erickson   Robert Harold Rosenquist

born 2/28/1938 in Oakland, CA   born 1/28/1936 in Oakland, CA
married "Bob" Rosenquist   married Connie Erickson
5/14/1960 in Visalia, CA   5/14/1960 in Visalia, CA

Children

John Erik
born 6/3/1961 in Sacramento
married Laura Janette Smith 7/30/1994 in San Francisco, CA

Karl Robert
born 9/4/1964 in San Jose, CA
died 7/11/2003 in Santiago Canyon, CA

Kurt Andrew
born 3/5/1970 in Baltimore, MD
died 8/1/1970 in Bel Air, MD

Kris Alexander
born 10/19/1970 in Baltimore, MD
married Toni Marie Dean 7/10/2001 in Portland, OR

Grandchildren (They call Bob "Bobo" and Connie "Gaby".)

Marin Kallie Rosenquist
born 9/25/1997 in Los Gatos, CA

John Anders Rosenquist
born 2/14/2000 in Los Gatos, CA

Alexander Karl Robert Rosenquist
born 12/29/2003 in Portland, OR

Erikson Dean Rosenquist
born 3/29/2006 in Portland, OR

Connie's parents (children's grandparents)

Mother: Sigrid Cecelia Lax
born 2/9/1912 in Seattle, WA
married John Roy Erickson 5/14/1932 in Stockton, CA
died 9/4/1987 in Visalia, CA

Father: John Roy Erickson
born 9/14/1911 in Replot, Finland
married Sigrid Cecelia Lax 5/14/1932 in Stockton, CA
died 8/29/1988 in Fullerton, CA

Connie's grandparents (children's great-grandparents)

Nana: Ida Johanna Andersson
born 2/16/1880 in Jacobstad, Finland
married Alexander Matthew Lax (Reipsar) 1/7/1911 in Eureka CA
died 3/16/1969 in Visalia, CA

Grandfather Lax: Alexander Matthew Lax
born 11/14/1878 in Finland
married Ida Anderson 1/7/1911 in Eureka, CA
died 11/10/1927 in Berkeley, CA

Gaby: Adelina Bjorkas Lena
born 5/23/1886 in Replot, Finland
married John Erick Erickson 9/29/1903 in San Francisco, CA
died 6/7/1977 in Visalia, CA

Papa: John Erick Erickson
born 9/18/1872 in Replot, Finland
married Lena Bjorkas   9/29/1903 in San Francisco, CA
died 9/2/1947 in Lodi, CA

Connie's great-grandparents (children's great-great-grandparents)

Gaby's mother: Ulla Eriksdotter Klavus
born 7/13/1860 in Replot, Finland
married Karl Erik Bjorkas
died 5/16/1922 in Replot, Finland

Gaby's father: Karl-Erik Karlsson Bjorkas
born 4/23/1860 in Replot, Finland
married Ulrika Klavus
died 4/4/1947 in Replot, Finland

Papa's mother: Eva Marie
born 1844 in Replot, Finland
married Eric Carlson Ojst
died 7/17/1908 in Replot, Finland

Papa's father: Eric Carlsson Ojst
born 8/26/1837 in Replot, Finland
married Eva Marie
died 1/21/1933 in Replot, Finland

Nana's mother: Anna Lena Mattsdotter
born 7/27/1855 in Jacobstad, Finland
married Jacob Andersson
died 12/12/1945 in Jacobstad, Finland

Nana's father: Jacob Andersson (Filpas)
born 7/18/1850 in Jacobstad, Finland
married Anna Mattsdotter
died 10/13/1919 (Worked in Orange, TX 1889–1914)

Grandfather Lax's mother: Lovisa
born ?
married Matts Johansson Reipsar (Laxback)
died 1/20/1885 in Karleby, Finland

Grandfather Lax's father: Matts Johansson Reipsar (Laxback)
born 7/6/1839 in Karleby, Finland
married Lovisa
died 11/10/1927 in Karleby, Finland

Connie's great-great-grandparents (children's great-great-great-grandparents)

Gaby's grandmother: Carisa Lisa Ericksdotter Kapell ˙
born 1/10/1837
married Karl Karlson Bjorkas

Gaby's grandfather: Karl Karlson Bjorkas
born 4/08/1836 in Replot, Finland
married Carisa Lisa Kapel

Papa's grandmother: Marie Sopjia Ojst
born 2/17/1808 in Replot, Finland
married Braham Jonasson Karf
died 2/20/1868 in Replot, Finland

Papa's grandfather: Braham Jonasson Karf
born 8/19/1807 in Replot, Finland
married Marie Ojst
died 11/12/1893 in Replot, Finland

Nana's grandmother: Greta Jacobsdoller
born 3/1/1824 in Jacobstad, Finland
married Matts Andersson (first marriage)
2/22/1846 in Jacobstad, Finland
died 7/20/1868 in Jacobstad, Finland

Nana's grandfather: Matts Andersson
born 7/14/1823
married Greta Jacobsdotter
2/1846 in Jacobstad, Finland
died 8/3/1903 in Jacobstad, Finland

Connie's great-great-great-grandparents
(children's great-great-great-great grandparents)

Gaby's great-grandmother: Margarita Andersdotter
born 8/15/1812
married Carl Jonasson Bjorkas

Gaby's great-grandfather: Carl Jonasson Bjorkas
born 11/02/1811 in Replot, Finland
married Magarita Andersdotter

Papa's great-grandmother: Brita Caisa Michelsdotter
born 8/26/1802 in Replot, Finland
married Eric Erickson Kapell (Gammal)

Papa's great-grandfather: Erik Erickson Gammal
born 3/10/1801 in Replot, Finland
married Brita Michelsdotter

Papa's great-grandmother: Catrina Delena Abrahamsdotter Klavus
born in Replot, Finland
married Erik Andersson Strahlman
died 4/11/1914 in Replot, Finland

Papa's great-grandfather: Erik Andersson Strahlman
born 1808 in Replot, Finland
married Catrina Klavus

Connie's great-great-great-great-grandparents
(children's great-great-great-great-great-grandparents)

Papa and Gaby's great-great-grandparents

Berta Mickelsdotter
born ?
married Anders Strahlman

Anders Strahlman
born 1779
married Berta Mickelsdotter

Maria "Maja" Lisa Andersdotter
born 1772
married Michael Johansson Nahls
died in Ronn

Michael Johansson Nahls
born 1768
married Maja Andersdotter
died 5/03/1823

Kaisa Lena Carlsdotter Berg
born 1/29/1781 in Sweden
married Johan Johansson Bjorkas
died in Replot, Finland

Johan Johansson Bjorkas
born 4/04/1789 in Replot, Finland
married Kaisa Berg

Maria Carlsdotter
born in Galt, Bjorko
married Anders Ersso (Erickson)
died 10/23/1822

Anders Erickson
born 1770
married Maria Carlsdotter
died 10/27/1822

Brita Lena Simonsdotter
born 1770
married Eric Gammal
died 3/27/1846

Eric Johansson (Gammal)
born 1770
married Brita Simonsdotter
died 7/21/1834 in Ronn, Sweden

Sigrid Jonasdotter
born 1736
married Jacob Strahlman
died 3/25/1850

Jacob Strahlman
born 1737
married Sigrid Jonasdotter
died 4/30/1808

Maria Andersdotters
born 1772 in Replot, Finland
married Michel Johansson Klavus
in Replot, Finland 6/3/1792

Michel Johansson Nahls Klavus
born 1768
married Maria Elisabeth "Maja" Andersdotter
in Replot, Finland 6/3/1792
died 5/3/1823

On Nana's side

Lisa Andersdotter
born 1767
married Matts Hansson

Matts Hansson
born in Kecko, Finland
married Lisa Andersdotter

Connie's great-great-great-great-great-grandparents
(children's great-great-great-great-great-great-grandparents)

Margarita Johansdotter
born ?
married Johann Farhrisson

Johan Farhrisson
born 1719
married Margarita Johansdotter
died 8/31/1732
They are parents of Michael Johansson Klavus.

Magdalena Carlsdotter
born 1746
married Anders Andersson

Anders Andersson
born 1726 in Ronn Finland
married Magdalena Carlsdotter
They are the parents of Anders Andersson

Anna Eriksdotter
born ?
married Elias Simonsson

Elias Simonsson
born ?
married Anna Eriksdotter
died 10/3/1747

Connie's great-great-great-great-great-great-grandparents
(children's great-great-great-great-great-great-great-grandparents)

Michelsdotter Bjorkas
born ?
married Simon Mattsson Mag

Simon Mattsson Mag
married ? Michelsdotter Bjorkas
died 1695

Bob's parents
(Ccildren's grandparents)

Mother: Ina Catherine Heinsen
born 2/11/ 2011 in Hames Valley, CA
married Harold Rosenquist 4/14/1934 in Oakland, CA
died 5/20/2000 in Pinole, CA

Father: Harold Elmer Rosenquist
born 3/21/1910 in Berkeley CA
married Ina Heinsen 4/14/1934 in Oakland, CA
died 10/31/1992 in Berkeley, CA

Bob's grandparents (children's great-grandparents)
They called their great grandmothers "Weeze" and "Suomi."

Ina's mother: Louise Josina Riewerts
born 5/02/1885 in Bradley, CA
married John Heinsen 4/06/1910 in Gonzales, CA
died 12/20/1967 in King City, CA

Ina's father: John Arthur Heinsen
born 2/14/1884 in Bradley, CA
married Louise Riewerts 4/06/1910 in Gonzales, CA
died 12/25/1956 in King City, CA

Harold's mother: Elizabeth"Betty" Sodergaard
born 9/15/1887 in Maxmo, Finland
married Elmer Rosenquist 3/20/1909 in Berkeley, CA
died 9/1989 in Berkeley, CA

Harold's father: Elmer Rosenquist
born 8/01/1886 in Scandia, Kansas
married Betty Sodergaard 3/20/1909 in Berkeley, CA
died 7/11/1956 in Berkeley, CA

Bob's great-grandparents (children's great-great-grandparents)

Ina's grandmother: Inna Katerina Knudsen
born 3/31/1860 in Ovenum, Fohr
married Broder Riewerts 6/22/1884 in San Francisco, CA
died 6/20/1942 in Oakland, CA

Ina's grandfather: Broder Jacob Riewerts
born 7/20/1965 in Ovenum, Fohr
married Inna Knudsen
died 7/20/1936 in Oakland, CA

Ina's grandmother: Ellen Jane "Nellie" MacDonagh
born 11/11/1862 in Ireland
married "Chris" Heinsen 4/18/1882 in Lockwood, CA
died 6/22/1929 in Lockwood, CA

Ina's grandfather: Christian Georg "Chris" Heinsen
born 2/10/1864 on Island of Fohr
married Nellie MacDonagh 4/18/1882 in Lockwood, CA
died 3/19/1922 in Lockwood, CA

Harold's grandmother: Anna Lisa Mattsdotter
born 9/11/1851 in Maxmo, Finland
married Jacob Sodergaard 5/18/1877 (2nd marriage of Anna Lisa)
died 9/13/1935 in Maxmo, Finland

Harold's grandfather: Jacob Sodergaard
born 1/06/1855
married Anna Mattsdotter
died 2/19/1935 in Maxmo, Finland

Harold's grandmother: Christine Rosenquist
born 4/03/1867 in Oslo, Norway
married ? and then Frank Damon
died 9/24/1936 in Berkeley, CA

Bob's great-great-grandparents (children's great-great-great-grandparents)

Harold's great-grandmother: Antonete Johansan
born 12/1838
married Christian Rosenquist
died 5/14/1907

Harold's great-grandfather: Christian Rosenquist
born 1834
married Antonete Johansan (second marriage)
died in Kansas 1/22/191

Harold's great-great-grandmother: Maja Stina Abbrahamsdotter
born 7/20/1811
married Abraham Mikelson

Harold's great-great-grandfather: Abraham Mikelson
born 3/19/1809
married Maja Abramsdotter

Ina's great-grandmother: Lena Christina Lolly
born 1/25/1821 in Wyk, Fohr
married Lorenz Knudsen in 1840
died 12/25/1901 in Ovenum, Fohr

Ina's great-grandfather: Lorenz Conrad Knudsen
born in 5/24/1819 on Ovenum, Fohr
married Lana Lolly in 1840
died 12/25/1901

Ina's great-grandmother: Louise Josina Lorenzen
born 8/22/1834
married Jan Riewerts in 1858
died 1919

Ina's great-grandfather: Jan Hinrich Riewerts
born 7/3/1834 in Ovenum, Fohr
married Louise Lorenzen in 1858
died 8/4/1900

Louise and Broder Riewert's parents. Broder attended the wedding in San Francisco of Inna Knudsen and his son Broder Riewerts.

Ina's great-grandmother: Mary Susan MacCloskkey
born 11/27/1825 in Cumber Clody, Ireland
married Edward MacDonough
died in Lockwood, CA 12/25/1906

Ina's great-grandfather: Edward MacDonough
born 1815 in Cumber Clody, Ireland
married Mary MacCloskey
died 1889 in Lockwood, CA

They immigrated in 1873, are the parents of Nellie MacDonough, and are buried at the Mission San Antonio in Jolon, CA.

Bob's great-great-great-grandparents
(children's great-great-great-grandparents)

Ina's great-great-grandmother: Mary ?
born 1782 in Cork, Ireland
married J. Thaddaeus MacDonagh (note spelling)
died in 1846

Ina's great-great-grandfather: J. Thaddaeus Mac Donagh
born 1/1777 in Cumber Clody, Ireland
married Mary ?

Ina's great-great-grandmother: Mary Quinn
Born ?
married Robert McCloskey

Ina's great-great-grandfather: Robert McClosky
born ?
married Mary Quinn

Ina's great-great-grandmother: Engelena Boysen
born ?
married Lorenz Lolly

Ina's great-great-grandfather: Lorenz Lolly
born ?
married Engelena Boysen
They were grandparents of Inna Riewerts and parents of Lena Lolly

Ina's great-great-grandmother: Keike Ohufs
born ?
married John Lorenzen

Ina's great-great-grandfather: John Heinrich Lorenzen
born ?
married Keike Olufs
They were parents of Louise Lorenzen

Ina's great-great-grandmother: Giente Mathiesen
born ?
married Jurgen Rarden

Ina's great-great-grandfather: Jurgen Young Barde
born ?
married Giente Mathiesen
They were parents of John Hinrich Riewerts.

Ina's great-great grandmother: Wehna Peters
born 1859
married Knud Broder Knudsen

Ina's great-great-grandfather: Knud Broder Knudsen
born 1845
married Weina Peters
died 1917 in Nyblum on Island of Fohr
They were grandparents of Lena Christina Lolly.

Bob's great-great-great-great-grandparents
(children's great-great-great-great-great-grandparents)

Ina's great-great-great-grandmother: Rosina Marin Hassold
born 1791
married Broder Knudson
died 1876

Ina's great-great-grandfather: Knute Broder Knudsen
born 1781
married Rosina Hassold

Ina's great grandmother: Mary Devine
born ?
married William McCloskey

Ina's great grandfather: William McCloskey
born ?
married Mary Devine

Ina's great grandfather: Hugh Quinn